LEDGE

JAMES NAPIER

Published by James Napier
©2011 James Napier
All rights reserved
ISBN 978-0-9571037-0-2

Designed by April Sky Design www.aprilsky.co.uk
Printed by GPS Colour Graphics Limited, Belfast

Acknowledgements

Thank you to everyone who helped in the development and production of this book. I am particularly grateful to all those who reviewed early drafts and provided valuable feedback. Special thanks to Gillian McGarry for editorial support.

It is impossible to read this book without gaining some understanding of Attention Deficit Disorder; that alone is reason enough for having written it.

All profits raised through the sale of this book will be donated to mental health charities.

For Michael

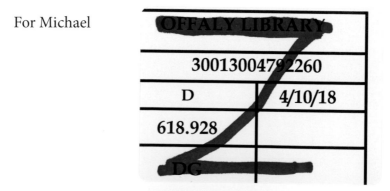

Prologue

The text alert thundered in, amplified by the lack of insulation between the ageing Nokia and the new oak worktop. Right on cue, I had been expecting a message from him sometime during the evening and nine o'clock was par for the course.

'Nothing more can be done. Up to date, report in from Carol Johnston this am. Refs in place. Morning prayers all that's left but lets hope for the best. Try not to worry cause we've all done our very best for Andrew on this. Talk to u tomorrow no matter wat!'

Should I let Sarah know that Rory had been in touch? Difficult to decide but in the end I let it sit. She would probably analyse every word when there wasn't really any subliminal message to analyse. Sleeping wasn't easy; so much rode on the next few hours.

As agreed, Sarah went to work on Wednesday. What was to be gained by her staying at home? I went myself for a couple of hours and then came home to pick Andrew up. He was almost ready but didn't know which of my suits to wear. Easy enough decision – there was probably only one that would fit and at least I knew where it was. Charcoal grey; seemed fairly apt.

The journey to Belfast was strange. We didn't talk much and it was hard to work out his form. He seemed OK but I couldn't be sure. Eventually we reached our destination. The car park was one of those old fashioned ones; above ground and built where an office block had been standing until a few months before. How long before the next monstrosity would be built on the site? Maybe longer than we thought, the credit crunch would see to that.

The parting was difficult. Father and son embraced. How long ago was it since we had done that? To my shame I couldn't remember. As he walked off, I couldn't look back, I was worried he might look round too. What was I going to do for the next few hours? How could I do anything? Still, it had been a long time since I had wandered aimlessly around the city. *Waterstones* was the first shop that caught my eye. I decided to investigate their popular science section. It was well laid out and well stocked and for most of the books on sale there seemed to be one copy only. No doubt a marvel of modern day stock control, all computer controlled and no wasted space. Perhaps the epitome of the risk free society – no metres of shelving devoted to books that wouldn't sell.

The new coffee dock was a welcome surprise. The regular Americano was still jumbo sized – what would a large cup have been like? It tasted good. All too aware of my reason for being in Belfast, I stationed my mobile on the edge of the table. Today, of all days, was not the day to miss a call through finding the right pocket. A cup of coffee could only last so long so eventually moved on, checking my bank account in the nearest hole in the wall. At least that didn't bring bad news; for once my estimation of how much was in the account was spot on. Not bad for two thirds through November.

Then it came. The familiar bleep of the phone started just as the sounds of the first Christmas song of the year drifted out of the shopping arcade just in front of me.

Chapter 1

January 1984 was a particularly bitter month and Wednesday 18th was especially tough. The apparently permanent snow and ice chilled the bones to the marrow, seemingly taunting the warm glow that the occasion should bring. The day had started badly enough; until lunchtime there was doubt as to whether I could be present. My boss had agonised over whether attending the birth of a second child was sufficient reason to be given the afternoon off work – how times have changed. It was typical of the time; little in the way of the employee rights that exist now.

Memories of that day, 25 years ago, are necessarily patchy. However, the memory of sitting in the car outside the maternity unit eating the still-frozen sandwiches that had been lifted from the freezer that morning remains crystal clear. My timing was good though, in a few hours number two would enter the world.

The delivery itself was reasonably straightforward even though 'high forceps' played their part somewhere along the way. At 3.35 pm Andrew entered the world, a County Tyrone child like his big sister, with the world at his feet.

There were no mobiles in those days and the news reached the grandparents through the familiar black bakelite hospital phones that had served new fathers for decades. 'It's a boy, mum.' 'Great, a nice surprise for his big sister', was the not unexpected answer. 'What are you going to call him?' I thought everyone knew what we were going to do. 'Andrew – Andrew Steven. Great that he's a boy – that evens things up. Nice for Suzanne too'.

One week later, the norm in those days – was this because

hospitals were less conscious of targets and budgets – mother and son returned to the family home. I of course, helped by my mother, had everything shipshape and ready for the returning entourage.

Things at home were not going to be easy; an older sibling of just over a year still brought demands that deprived working parents of sleep and energy. Number two would have to share the nursery, still in a resplendent pink. The prospect of long sleepless nights again only slightly dulled the joy that the second child had brought. We were young enough to cope with the wear and tear. Anyway this is what young parents did.

Andrew was an idyllic child; he slept when you wanted him to and he fed well. That is until he was about two. From then on it appeared as if he didn't need to sleep, particularly during the night – I often wished that I had a motor as good as his. It was during these long nights that I became an expert with *Meccano* and *Lego* and was unsure as to whether I would have been better served had I entered employment as an architect or engineer as opposed to being a teacher. The *Meccano* tool kit came in handy to replace the screws that he would remove from the bedroom furniture. It was many years later that the significance of having a budding carpenter aged two would become fully apparent. I did though marvel at the dexterity of a two year old in removing screws and hinges from all around him. Why did he do it?

Life was hard but good and like many other young parents we were facing the age – old quandary. Should Sarah remain at work or stay at home to look after the children. In the end it was decided that she would stop working for a few years. This was a difficult decision because it would bring huge financial pressures. Living on one junior teacher's salary might do but there would be no room for luxuries. However, we were convinced that having a parent at home and bringing up the children in their own surroundings would give them the best start in life. And anyhow, child care, even in those days, was patchy in quality and certainly not cheap.

The months and years merged with first Suzanne starting school and then in September 1988, Andrew was the age to join the local primary school.

He looked the part in his new school uniform with his bright red tie contrasting sharply with the white shirt and blue jumper. It was a tough beginning to formal education as he was still very immature; still a baby. Organisation was not his forte; probably a boy thing.

My first real memory of his education was from half way through his first term. Andrew had only been in the school a couple of months when he had to be collected early one day – I can't remember the reason, it could have been a doctor's appointment or anyone of a hundred other reasons. Unusually it was I who went into the classroom to collect him. Entering the classroom was commonplace enough – parents of P1 children tended to float in and out throughout the day. The era of locked doors and CCTV had still not become part of primary school life.

The P1 classroom was spacious and the pupils sat in groups of four with two pairs of desks arranged to face each other. The desks and chairs were elf sized and just right for four and five year olds. When I arrived Andrew seemed frozen to his seat and appeared oblivious to my presence, or for that matter his teacher asking him to pack away his books when she saw me arrive. Eventually he did manage to get organised but not before one or two of the other pupils had a quiet snigger at his attempts to find his lunch box and outdoor shoes. The whole episode took no more than about five minutes but it seemed an eternity. I couldn't wait to get out of the place.

For some reason I felt a cold shiver run through me as we departed and I couldn't get the image of Andrew as a victim out of my mind for the rest of the day. What was I basing this on? – precious little – but the thought wouldn't leave me for some time.

Progress at school appeared to be satisfactory over the next few years. We weren't getting the dreaded phone calls or letters requesting a meeting with the Principal and there was no more red pen than expected on his class or home work. Everything drifted on until that crisis – precipitating individual, the inflexible substitute teacher, arrived on the scene.

Mrs Smith was forty-something, and had an appearance as anonymous as her name. She arrived for what was initially a four week stay to cover for Andrew's teacher who was ill with what we all guessed was a stress-related condition – she had that look, emaciated and anxious, the type that stress was invented for. It was never expressed in these terms to us as parents but this was what everyone knew – country schools kept few secrets.

Mrs Smith had a voice that could penetrate walls. I just knew that trouble was on the horizon. It took about a month for the 'Mr Moore, can I have a word' to come from the Principal as I was doing the afternoon collection. 'We have had a bit of trouble today', 'Oh, Yes'. 'I'm afraid Andrew assaulted another child in his class today'. 'Assaulted' was as much as I could gasp as my voice faded with the horror. 'He tripped Janine Willis and she fell and cut her leg – nothing serious – but her mother is very unhappy and insisting that Andrew is punished'. 'What are you going to do?' I said. 'Keep him in detention on Friday, but I should say that Andrew's behaviour has been causing some concern. We cannot get him to focus for any length of time and he is so easily distracted, not to mention distracting the other children.'

On the way home little was said. Hardly any point with four of us in the car. I decided I would pick my moment later. Andrew and I walked to the shop as Sarah made the tea. 'Andrew, why did you trip Janine? Was it an accident?' 'I don't know why I tripped her, no reason'. 'No reason, for God's sake, you could have badly hurt her'. 'I know, but I just couldn't help it.' We clearly were not going to get too far so I let it drop; it was much easier to talk about how the football had gone at lunch time. Maybe I was opting out but it seemed the best path for now.

After this fiasco, school trundled on without too many major disasters but nonetheless with a slight undercurrent of all not being totally well. Just enough to keep me on edge, but not enough to make me do anything about it.

At least Suzanne was making good progress. She was near the top of her class and got a grade A in her transfer test in P7. She was to transfer from the primary to the local Grammar School in September. She had proved to be an idyllic child, no trouble and bright to boot. She barely needed any parenting at all, it all seemed so effortless.

With Suzanne in 'big school' Andrew's final years at primary school were geared to preparation for the same dreaded transfer test that she had sailed through. This was the test that determined the fate of eleven years olds and identified them as being suitable for a selective Grammar School education or a non-selective secondary education. In reality between thirty and forty percent of the pupils taking the test would get a high enough grade to guarantee them the Grammar School of their choice. In many families the parents took the test, and the preparation which invariably included individual coaching, more seriously than their children. Perhaps they knew just how much was often riding on the two tests that took place in the autumn term of P7. Even the mothers of those high-flying pupils who were certain to get a grade A (certain to everyone bar themselves) managed to get themselves highly stressed and worked up. It's not hard to see why the Government saw off the transfer tests.

Andrew was fairly nonplussed about the whole thing; like everyone else he agreed to be taken to his tutor for the obligatory one hour's coaching each week in the final few months before the tests. The tutor, like everyone else, thought that Andrew was on the borderline between grades A and B. This of course did matter as in the part of the country where we lived a grade B was no springboard to a Grammar School place, and certainly not the one we wanted him to go to.

The dates of the tests approached and we thought that Andrew was as well prepared as he could be – more past papers could have been pored over but there is *always* more one can do – until D-Day arrived.

The pupils involved were allowed home after they had completed the test. Some parents organised 'parties' – a bit over the top after only the first test I thought – but Sarah, now back in full-time work and on maternity leave with number three, took Andrew for his lunch instead. He has a voracious appetite – always had – and remained as thin as a rake; reflecting on this Sarah could only feel jealous; like most women she had to work at staying trim.

Naturally there was the debriefing but it was very difficult to get anything of significance from him. 'It was OK and I did get it finished, apart from the last page' was as much as we could get. 'How much was on the last page and how did you know it was only the last page?' was the obvious retort. Still there is not a lot to be gained by post-mortems, especially as they may have no bearing on the reality of the performance.

Anyhow, it all worked out fine. Andrew got a grade A – I suspect by the skin of his teeth – and he was destined for the same Grammar School that his elder sister was at. What more could parents want?

Chapter 2

The reward for finishing primary school, and working hard for the transfer test, was a trip to London. Andrew was to continue the tradition started when his sister had completed her primary schooling. Memories of that trip came flooding back, the excitement of visiting Madame Tussauds, the Museum of the Moving Image on the South Bank and a host of other must-do sights. I had gone with Suzanne on her own, Sarah staying at home with Andrew. She thought it would be a good opportunity for some 'father-daughter bonding' and it was.

The same arrangements stood for Andrew's three or four day visit to the capital. The timing worked particularly well as I was employed as an Open University residential schools tutor during the last week of July at Reading University. The plan was that Andrew and I would fly out together on the Tuesday or Wednesday beforehand and we would have a few days doing the things tourists do before he would fly back unaccompanied on the Saturday allowing me to travel down to Reading.

We ended up flying out first thing on Wednesday morning and planned to stay in Uxbridge with an elderly aunt. Heathrow to Uxbridge was no distance and finding our welcoming accommodation was relatively straightforward as Suzanne and I had taken the same route only two years earlier.

Madame Tussuads was to take place on the Thursday morning. Being a 'veteran' now of such trips I had worked out that advance credit card booking avoided the indeterminable queues of cosmopolitan tourists that perpetually snaked along the pavements of this premier tourist attraction. The visit itself quickly degenerated into a battle of wills. It was not long before it became apparent that Andrew wanted to use the entire roll in his disposable camera in that one building. 'Andrew do you not think that you might want to keep some of the film for the Natural History or Science Museums?' 'No, I want to use it all now'. 'Why?' 'Because I want to use it now.'

A similar scenario existed with his money. If I hadn't restrained him he would have spent all his money by Thursday morning. Budgeting and planning ahead were distant goals that were well beyond where we were at. I knew all too well that Hamley's would be where he would really want to spend his money. Difficult to spend if he didn't have any left!

These might seem like little things and no doubt at least partially attributable to the slower maturation of boys compared to girls. Nonetheless, there were just too many little things that didn't appear to be just right or was I over reacting? Surely a trip to Madame Tussuads shouldn't be stressful? This took me back to the first time we had concerns about Andrew. It was around the time of the long sleepless nights building *Meccano* trucks and *Lego* villages. 'Let's take him to the doctor', Sarah had suggested then, after a particular difficult night. 'After all he is two years old'.

Visiting the GP with fairly nebulous concerns was not easy. 'What are we going to say, Sarah?' 'Say we are concerned – we are parents and have been through it before. We know that something is different, not right, don't we?' It is not that we had tremendous faith in our GP finding anything or had any real hope that we would come away satisfied but we did have nagging doubts.

The GP listened patiently but with a knowing look. He of course had seen it all before, the anxious, over-worried parents.

'What do you expect toddlers to do but keep their parents awake half the night and what was odd about dismantling the bedroom furniture?' He offered to make a referral – only too delighted to pass these nutcases on to someone else.

As with many non-urgent referrals there was no point in holding our breath and it was never made clear exactly who the referral was to. It was anyone's guess as far as I was concerned. I wasn't going to hold my breath for a speedy outcome. I thought the best thing to do was to forget about the whole thing; things would sort themselves out in the end.

About three months later the buff envelope with the give-away transparent window arrived. We tended not to get too many letters like that then. The only official letters we seemed to get were from the bank and they came in a distinctive long white envelope. I often thought that they should put a nice red boundary round the envelope just to finish it off – bank letters were seldom good news. We had an appointment in a few weeks and they wanted to see Andrew and both his parents. In fact it was to be with a psychologist. I knew a bit about psychology; it was a subject I had considered for university and I often regretted that I hadn't pursued that particular route. I had read 'around the subject' as they say and was informed enough to consider whether it was going to be a child psychologist or an educational psychologist. Sarah and I debated this point. 'If he is coming to our house then it must be a clinical psychologist, mustn't it? Surely educational psychologists work in schools.' I couldn't answer, I wasn't sure.

It turned out to be an educational psychologist. He was quite young, around about our age, and possibly the thinnest adult I had ever met. He tested Andrew with a few toys and games and checked reflexes and other motor functions. I couldn't help feel that we were being tested as well – what did he expect, parents with two heads? After about 30 minutes he had finished his routine. It seemed particularly regimented and he appeared to refer to his books a lot. Did he have to carry everything out in a particular order? 'I think your son is fine, Mr and Mrs Moore, nothing to worry about. In fact there is some evidence that he may be gifted'. 'What exactly does gifted mean?' I asked. 'His performance in a few of the tests was at a higher level than could be expected for someone of his age.' When the visit was over I felt slightly despondent. Really we were no further on but what did we expect. Perhaps we were feeling guilty about bringing a busy educational psychologist out to the house on flimsy grounds. Yes, the sooner this episode was over the better and we could get back to reality.

The rest of the London trip was fine. Andrew had settled down a bit and was calmer. Had I over reacted? The Natural History and Science Museums were as much for my benefit as his – we hadn't visited these during Suzanne's visit and it had been many years before I had wandered round the majestic skeleton of *T. rex* and marvelled at the cut -away section of the jumbo jet. Perhaps I was benefitting from a touch of escapism.

The rest of the summer holidays passed in a daze. The weather seemed so much better then. No talk of global warming or climatic Armageddon. School uniforms were purchased and the start of the new term loomed as it did for so many families. How would we all cope when Andrew started the big school in September? We were soon going to find out the answer to that riddle.

Chapter 3

A family friend, a senior teacher in a local school, once suggested that if new pupils could keep their heads down and stay 'under the radar' until the October half term they would turn out all right. 'The really bad ones float to the top within the first two or three weeks' he had said somewhat sardonically; no doubt a comment based on years of experience. Subconsciously, Halloween became our target – no trouble before then and we were going to be OK.

We nearly made it. Detention on the day the school broke up was pretty close. The pro-forma letter stated that the offence was "inappropriate behaviour in the classroom". Hardly that illuminating. It turned out that a dispute had arisen over a learning homework. Andrew had claimed that the homework had never been set. 'Andrew, surely not doing a learning homework would not get you a detention. Was there something else?' 'Not really'. 'Why did she actually put you in detention?' 'For not doing my homework', he continued to answer. Following a phone call to the school it transpired that the 'offence' was not, not doing the homework – although this was not the first time apparently – but insisting that the teacher didn't set it, even though everyone else in the class had completed it, or so I was told.

During the rest of the year there were two other detentions. Not for particularly serious breaches of school discipline but an accumulation of minor indiscretions.

Not that the year was all gloom and doom. Andrew had

thrown himself into the sporting life of the school. He was an enthusiastic, if not brilliant, rugby player. He was just too small and didn't have the lightening speed or acrobatic agility required to compensate. Most of the time he also appeared reasonably happy and in most subjects he appeared to be coping OK.

Life at home was starting to be coloured by Andrew's tendency to act impulsively and there appeared little doubt that 'his mouth and his brain were not working in tandem'. Often this just passed as a minor irritation but you could start to sense the unease, the waiting for the bombshell, from whatever source. Sarah had had enough, her patience was wearing thin. 'We need some support. Why can't anyone tell us what is wrong?' I had no answer. Leafing through the *Yellow Pages* we found the name of a clinical psychologist (Dr J Johnston – chartered clinical psychologist - specialising in family relationships and adolescence behaviours, the block advert told us). He seemed the pick of what was on offer, largely because he was within easy driving range. Ringing the number listed, it became apparent that he worked from home and following a brief outline of why we wanted to see him an appointment was made for the following week.

The directions to his house proved straightforward and easy to follow. No 'sat nav' in those days. The house itself was a long L shaped bungalow, typical of well – to – do, suburbia in smaller towns. Dr Johnston greeted us himself after the first chime of the doorbell. Was there a Mrs Johnston – difficult to tell? After the initial preamble, we got down to business. 'Tell me your concerns – from the very beginning. It will help me build up a picture'. For about ten minutes we filled in the details, each one perhaps insignificant on its own. He was good at probing, asking for more. To our surprise, he then focused on us. 'Tell me Sarah – we were on first name terms – do you and Peter always work out agreed strategies to deal with Andrew'. Sarah answered, 'Do you mean generally, or do you mean do we work out an agreed strategy after something has happened?' 'Both'. 'We try to be consistent but it is not always easy, Andrew seems expert at identifying when even there is the slightest disagreement between us.' And so on.

I couldn't help get the feeling that we were on the psychiatrist's couch. It was us in the spotlight. Eventually he was ready to give us some feedback – the answers to our prayers? 'I think you have a very lively and difficult to manage child, but well within the normal norms. Would you like me to see him?' 'Why? What would you do?' 'I could see him to confirm my opinions and perhaps give you some advice on parenting strategies'. At last, I thought, he is coming out with it. We are the ones at fault. We received some advice on 'managing difficult children' and the need for 'consistency.' We agreed that we would think about coming back to see him in a few weeks.

A few minutes after handing over the £45 cheque I knew I wouldn't be back.

Other aspects of life were progressing well. Both Sarah and I were now in careers that gave us satisfaction, if not always the rewards we thought we deserved. Like many people we worked hard to ensure that our respective careers allowed some quality family time. Suzanne was making good progress at school and the breadth of her extra-curricular involvement showed her to be to be well balanced and a solid member of the school and local communities. For long stretches of time life really wasn't too bad at all. But we still had the GCSE years to get through – a crunch time with adolescents in general. I knew that for Andrew it was a time that had the potential to be catastrophic. 'I could feel it in my bones', as my mother would say.

Chapter 4

Fourth Form (or Year 11 in modern currency) promised to be a nightmare. By the time Andrew had finished Third Form we were clearly entering uncharted waters. He was reluctant to attend school; not all of his friends were the children you wanted your child to associate with and it was obvious we had problems beyond the normal range of adolescent behaviours. I could predict the likely outcomes – school suspension or even expulsion, alcohol, drugs or trouble with the police. It was just a matter of what and when and in which order.

His journey through school became increasingly chaotic. The list of issues was endless – difficult relationships with peers, with teachers, and a total inability to remain focused in even the most engaging of classes. As with many children with 'problems' he did relate well to some teachers but had very volatile relationships with others. A perceptive onlooker could predict in advance which teachers would be in each category. He became increasingly present on the fringe of 'incidents', if not actually directly involved. It was also evident that success in the GCSE examinations themselves would be limited. However, we were realistic enough to recognise that they were the least of our problems.

At home he became increasing troublesome. Relationships with other members of the family became fractious and we became immersed in a bubble of tension and developing hopelessness.

At this time it became very apparent that Andrew's

impulsiveness, added to his apparent inability to stay within the boundaries of what we regarded as appropriate behaviour, were hampering his ability to have normal relationships. His inability to empathise with others was becoming increasingly marked and obvious. He couldn't sit at peace – he had to be fiddling, messing or creating havoc in some form or other.

One particular incident, while not being atypical, sums up the point of despair we had reached. Sarah and I had arranged to meet an old school friend for lunch. The restaurant had been booked for a particular time and we were dropping Andrew off with a friend of his on the way. He was playing one of his computer games on the PC as we were getting ready. This was another symptom; he could play with the one game for hours and hours, totally engrossed to the exclusion of all else. I think the game was a computer version of *Battleships and Cruisers*. We were starting to run late and Andrew wouldn't leave the game. He appeared to be barely aware that I was asking him to stop and was becoming increasingly desperate. My pleading continued for what seemed ages but was probably about ten minutes. Eventually I cracked and switched the computer off at the plug and grabbed him by the arm moving him in the direction of the car. The explosion that resulted ended with him kicking a hole in the study door and a tirade of abusive language that must have carried through the village. I also lost control and was lucky that I only punched him on the arm. It brought tears but I was all too aware that I could have really hurt him. As he sat crying at the kitchen table I could sense that he couldn't comprehend why there had been confrontation. What were we facing? Guilt cast a long shadow over the day's events.

We did make our rendezvous, only slightly late, but in a state where relaxation and a genuine enjoyment of the meal and company was a forlorn hope.

Sarah was not coping very well. She was often agitated and clearly suffering from stress. Our own relationship started to be tested. Rows could erupt from nowhere and for little reason.

At our wits end, we made another appointment to see the GP. After all it had been some years before we were down this path before. Surely something could be done this time. Everyone could see that we had a real problem on our hands. We made the appointment – that was the easy part. We were going to see the GP on our own – we didn't even have to try and persuade Andrew to accompany us.

We both entered the consulting room. Dr Willets, an open faced man who was probably only slightly older than ourselves, closed the door gently. We quickly explained why we had come; perhaps trying to justify why two healthy people were using one of his valuable slots. 'You are OK', he said. 'I have an interest in mental health problems. I considered being a psychiatrist before opting for the GP route. Yes, I regard myself as a bit of an expert in this field. I can tell whether someone is suffering from mental illness.' I wasn't sure what to make of this. Not being a doctor, I didn't want to comment on his suggestions but I did think that one of those 'syndromes' that Andrew was probably suffering from might be a bit more difficult to diagnose than he thought. Still, he did give us time and showed genuine concern. He was aware that we, as parents, were suffering. Yes, the way forward was to see Andrew next. 'Please make an appointment on the way out with the receptionist'.

One week later we returned with Andrew in tow. He was acquiescent enough but his body language didn't exactly exhibit enthusiasm. The plan was for Andrew to go first and then Dr Willets would see us all together. Andrew was in for about ten minutes – was that a good sign? He came out scowling. We entered the consulting room in trepidation. What were we going to hear? 'I have had a good look at Andrew and you will be pleased to know he hasn't a serious mental condition. I have also given him a good talking to and made clear to him he is worrying his parents'. Was this it? I knew he hadn't paranoia or one of the major mental illnesses. I knew the next step wasn't becoming an inpatient at the local psychiatric unit. More of the bleeding obvious. Sarah asked 'What happens next?' more in desperation than hope. 'If you would like I will put him on the waiting list to see the child psychiatrist who works at the local children's out-centre. He is an expert in this field. However, there is probably a waiting list of about six months. He is in great demand'. No wonder, I thought.

Although only fifteen, Andrew was becoming part of what is referred to in legal or political jargon as the 'underclass culture'. Snooker halls and gaming joints became familiar haunts. His 'friends' were often transient and he was all too familiar with alcohol. He appeared to be on a downward spiral and there was nothing we could do to stop it. He began staying out overnight and when he did he often switched his mobile phone off, despite what we had agreed. I couldn't even confirm that he was all right. It was around that time that he had his first brush with the police.

Saturday afternoons were invariably spent 'in town'. In town involved playing snooker or a similar activity and ending up in a friend's house; usually one where the parents were away. Often there weren't parents as such; usually a single parent or other relative was theoretically in charge. At around nine o'clock on one such night the dreaded heavy knock on the door arrived. Andrew was brought home by the police, suspected of underage drinking. He had come to the notice of the police as he 'staggered' along the pavement as part of a 'ropey looking crowd'. In retrospect, the attention-inducing gait was influenced by a rugby injury picked up that morning – thankfully he still took part in some 'normal' activities that allowed us to cling to some hope. He had been drinking – he admitted as much – but it wasn't particularly obvious. The passing shot of the young police officer who did most of the talking was that there would probably be a follow-up visit in due course. 'The juvenile liaison officer will make an appointment to call and see you and Andrew. He might get a juvenile caution. Depends what they think is best'. If Andrew had been drinking earlier in the day, it was me that needed one now. Sarah also needed some succour – she had her glass poured before the police car had left the drive. What really was sad, was that neither of us could provide any real comfort for each other. We just didn't know what we could do. I couldn't wave any magic wands.

I knew immediately the envelope hit the floor what it was. The appointment with the child psychiatrist had come. On cue; almost exactly six months after we had our meeting with the GP.

Dr Harris was well known as an expert in his field – well known to those who had reason to find out. I suspect most parents had no idea of who he was or had the slightest inkling of the complexities of his work. He appeared to be of eastern European descent although exactly where was difficult to conclude. Working with children was obviously his forte; his ability to relate to this age group was evident from the start. Reassurance oozed from every pore; it was difficult not to feel optimistic; not to feel that at last we might be getting somewhere. He subtly emphasised that that his relationship was with Andrew; we were bit-players. I liked his psychology.

'Andrew, do you know why you have come to see me?' 'I think so'. He gently added, 'Well then, tell me why you think you are here'. 'My parents think I need to see someone' was the predictable response. 'Andrew, you know there is more to it than that'. 'Yes, I do, but I'm not sure what it is. I just think that something is wrong somewhere'. 'That's why you are here Andrew. We want to try to find out if there is a problem. More importantly if there is one, we would like to put it right. Wouldn't you?'

Dr Harris had us almost spellbound. He was the first adult that we had seen Andrew engage with, engage with properly, for some time. Certainly it was proving to be a very positive first meeting.

'Andrew, I would like you to see one of my colleagues. Are you happy to do this?' 'Why can you not see me?' was Andrew's slightly uncertain response. 'I will see you again - you are my patient, but I would like Dr Warden to carry out a few tests. She is a clinical psychologist, an excellent one, and at the top of her profession. Will you see her?' 'Yes' 'Good, I will get your first meeting arranged within the next two weeks. It would be useful if at least one of your parents could come along although they will not be part of the tests. It is important that they know what is going on and are there to support you'.

At last we seemed to be getting somewhere. What would the tests show?

Chapter 5

Andrew had three one hour sessions with Dr Warden; she also had two half hour sessions with Sarah and me; I assume to get as much background information as she could.

Our first session with Dr Warden was particularly harrowing. Sarah spent much of it in tears; the toll of the previous years coupled with the probing retrospective nature of the meeting saw to that. Clinical psychologists must by necessity probe the depths. The mood wasn't lifted when Dr Warden explained that 'the intervention required will be dependant on the extent of family dysfunction.' This comment was particularly hard to take; yet in many ways in was right. It was impossible to function as a normal family amidst the turmoil. We did try, but if we were honest, normality wasn't always within our remit. Still, the words were yet another hammer blow.

Andrew almost seemed to enjoy the sessions. He talked about doing this test or that test and how he was able to work out the answers. Though, he did think it was daft asking him to read a passage from a book and count the number of times a bell rang during his reading. 'Sure a child could do this. I don't see what the purpose is.' 'No Andrew, I cannot either' I said. It made me think though. Was this an exercise on Andrew's ability to multi-task? What has this got to do with his behavioural problems?'

After Andrew's third session, Dr Warden said that she still had to write up the report but would be willing to discuss interim conclusions with us if we wished to. 'Yes, of course we would'. We headed into her small office; the poor lighting not adding to any sense of space. When she began speaking, her words were measured and soft. 'I think we have discovered that Andrew has problems relating to his ability to concentrate and remain focused. It seems, and this has to be confirmed, that he has the condition 'Attention Deficit Disorder or ADD. Have you heard of this condition?' We answered almost in tandem. 'Is it not called Attention Deficit Hyperactive Disorder or ADHD? We were familiar with that term; it had been a term that was beginning to be used in education, usually in association with a particularly disruptive pupil. 'No', she replied. 'I think the variety of the condition Andrew has is one without the hyperactivity. Some children have the hyperactive form and some have it without the hyperactive element, though in other aspects the condition is the same'. Andrew might have been hyperactive at one time but he doesn't fit the pattern now.

This information brought mixed emotions. Certainly there was some understanding now but we knew it was a condition that couldn't simply be switched off. The word 'syndrome' sprung to mind and not for the first time.

Dr Warden then outlined some of the key features of the condition. She did explain that it was a condition that had only really begun to enter the public domain and even within the medical profession there was still considerable uncertainty. 'ADD is basically a problem with brain chemistry. Sufferers find it very hard to concentrate; they can often focus on one task but the concept of multi-tasking is usually beyond them', she continued. Soaking this information up I was thinking that the pieces were beginning to fall into place' or at least some of them were. There were questions that I was burning to ask. Dr Warden continued, 'children with ADD are very impulsive. The concept of delayed gratification is too difficult for them. Everything must be done at once. Unfortunately, children have the condition from birth and it your son's case it has take nearly sixteen years to get a diagnosis. In that time emotional development has been stymied, and almost invariably self-esteem is very low. However all is not lost as there is something we can do.' This triggered my response. 'What can you do? 'Dr Harris will discuss this with you. There are a number of options. Behavioural therapy and drug treatment are two possibilities but it is better you discuss this with him. I'll make an appointment for the three of you to see him as soon as he has an available appointment.'

Leaving the Health Centre our minds were racing but we didn't discuss much on the way home; Andrew was in the car. There was much to discuss though.

It took nearly three weeks for the appointment with Dr Harris to arrive. Within that window we had enough time to realise that knowledge of the problem doesn't necessarily solve the problem. Why did we think it could? Perhaps this realisation didn't allow us to meet Dr Harris in a more upbeat mood. Still it was good to be at the next stage.

Dr Harris as always addressed Andrew first. He was clearly up to date on the details of the psychologist's report. After the usual initial niceties he briefly summarised the report's findings. His feedback was lucid and tightly worded; no words wasted. Clearly, a man at the height of his powers. He proposed that Andrew start a course of medicine; a drug that would act to curb his impulsiveness and allow him to focus more easily.

'Andrew are you willing to take this drug?' Andrew hesitated, perhaps thinking did he really have an option. 'Yes, I will. What is it like? Will it muddle my brain?' Dr Harris explained in detail the virtue of the drug in 'Andrew language' – he clearly was expert in dealing with children. No wonder he had a very high reputation within the health service.

The drug was Ritalin. It should be taken twice a day. Dr Harris wrote the prescription on the spot. He did finish by saying though, 'it doesn't work for everyone and it may take a while before we get the correct dose sorted out. There is an element of trial and error at this stage. However, you should see some benefit fairly quickly'. 'How quickly', I asked. 'Oh, within days. It really works that fast. I'll make another appointment for about four weeks time to see how things are going. We can also look at other options as well as the drugs – they may not be the whole answer – in fact they are unlikely to be'.

As we left Dr Harris' consulting room we were met by a young mother and a child, a young boy aged about eight I thought, who was obviously next on his list. I couldn't help thinking if this child also had ADD or ADHD, and if he did, how much better his chances were than a child diagnosed at fifteen. The wasted years made me feel angry.

Chapter 6

The next few weeks were spent scouring the Internet and the libraries for information about ADD or ADHD. There was no shortage of information. My first surprise was that it is a condition that has been well documented for a considerable period of time.

It seems that the condition was first described by a Dr Heinrich Hoffman in the middle eighteen hundreds and the story of "Fidgety Philip" recounted the behaviours of a little boy who had the condition now known as ADHD. In the early part of the Twentieth Century the famous English paediatrician, Sir George Still, probably became the first British medical practitioner to describe the condition. In a lecture to the Royal College of Physicians he described a group of children with the behavioural difficulties now associated with ADD but where the symptoms could not be attributed to poor parenting and therefore must have had a biological basis.

During the second half of the Twentieth Century more and more medical practitioners and academics pursued their research in this area. With up to five percent of the population being affected, according to the research, it is not surprising that there is a growing interest in the condition.

ADHD / ADD sufferers show the key symptoms of inattention, impulsivity and sometimes hyperactivity. These tend to appear early in a child's life and to be ADHD / ADD related they must be present to a greater extent and for a longer duration than the typical childhood norms.

The Diagnostic and Statistical Manual of Mental Disorders (DSM-IV-TR), criteria established by the American Psychiatric Association, provide a broad set of criteria that can be used for diagnosis. Other criteria have been developed in other countries and general guidelines exist that can help practitioners identify if further research should be undertaken, when the condition is suspected. The main symptoms are relatively easy to recognise but it is much more difficult to establish if their degree of presentation is beyond the norm; particularly as there will be such variation in children. The inattention symptom itself can be confusing as the child can focus if the task in hand is one they enjoy. In fact they can be almost obsessive if they are interested – cue *Battleships and Cruisers*. Impulsiveness is seen in the inability to show control or the inability to delay immediate gratification for perhaps greater long term gain and the hyperactive child is just that, always on the go and looking for something else to do.

As the symptoms of inattention, impulsivity and hyperactivity are inappropriate behaviours in school, the first regular formal setting for most children, it is not surprising that the condition is most frequently diagnosed in Primary School with a typical age of around seven or eight. Why did we miss it then? Surely there was enough evidence?

It is one thing identifying if the condition exists, but what actually causes it? As with many conditions, progress is being made but not to the extent where a definitive cause has been identified. What is known is that ADHD has a definite neurobiological basis; it is associated with deficiencies with neurotransmitters; with dopamine being perhaps most affected. Neurotransmitters are the chemicals that link different neurones in the nervous system (most of which are found in the brain). Normally the nervous system conducts information through electrical pulses (nerve impulses) that pass along neurones (specialised nerve cells). The electrical signals cannot cross the gaps between neurones so the chemical neurotransmitters serve to transmit information at these junctions.

ADHD also tends to run in families; if one member of a family has the condition there is a significant chance that a sibling will have it – much greater than there would be for a member of the general public. If one identical twin has the condition the other one usually does. This virtually proves that it is genetically inherited or at the very least a genetic pre-disposition. Research is continuing trying to identify which gene, or genes, are involved. However, as with other chronic conditions such as diabetes, it is likely that a number of genes are involved, each to a different extent, making the identification of the genes primarily responsible very difficult. I knew that this was one area to steer clear off when discussing ADD with Sarah. Nothing was going to be gained by trying to work out which side of the family had contributed the faulty genes. There is evidence to suggest that the gene complex affected overlaps with the gene complex associated with the conditions broadly summarised as autistic spectrum disorders.

Results arising from twin studies are very interesting. Twin studies are often used to determine how much genetics affects particular conditions. If a condition is purely genetic then if one identical twin has the condition the other identical twin will invariably be affected as identical twins have the same genes – they both develop from the same egg and sperm following conception.

Research in identical twins with ADD show that if one twin has the condition there is around about an eighty percent chance that the other twin will have it. Certainly this is very strong evidence that genetics is the key factor in the condition's incidence but it is not the whole story or it would be 100%. Recent research suggests that while the two twins have the same genetic makeup the effects of the relevant genes, or their 'expression' to use the biological term in one twin can be influenced by environmental conditions. There is speculation as to what these environmental conditions could be but there are suggestions that stresses created by different experiences in the womb could play a part. The consequence is that the genes responsible for the onset of ADD operate in a slightly different way in a twin with ADD than the same genes do in the other twin that doesn't have the condition. This again highlights the complexity of the genetic causes of the condition and also the difficulties in developing genetic cures such as gene therapy.

Some researchers propose that the gene mutations responsible mutated or evolved at a time when humans were hunter gatherers and not the relatively sophisticated species we are now. At that time impulsiveness or hyperactivity may have encouraged a degree of inventiveness or innovation useful in that environment. The mutant variation of the gene may have been beneficial then and this could account for its relatively widespread distribution in the population today. Certainly some individuals with ADD today can find success through high levels of creativity, but for most it is an unwelcome millstone.

It is also much more common in boys – possibly because men were the hunter gatherers. It is also very probable that girls are under-diagnosed due to girls being more likely to show the inattentive characteristics of the condition as opposed to the more noticeable impulsive and hyperactive sides. Inattention will not cause the same disruption in schools or family homes therefore there will be less pressure on finding a diagnosis or medical or other solutions.

Although a neurobiological condition with a strong genetic

trait, there is little doubt that environmental factors can exacerbate, if not cause ADHD. Weak parenting and the inability to set boundaries as a child grows up will certainly compound problems stemming from hyperactive and impulsive behaviour. This may help explain why the uninformed cynically dismiss the condition as the out-workings of poor parenting. There have been suggestions that environmental agents such as lead pollution and cigarette smoking or drinking alcohol during pregnancy shows a positive correlation with ADHD incidence but the results are inconclusive. Reading this wasn't uplifting either. We were not weak parents, but paid very heavily for any little chinks in our management. It really is a bastard of a condition.

Medication can be used to help treat or manage the symptoms of ADHD. For many years, stimulants have been used. It is thought that the stimulants such as amphetamine or methylphenidate (Ritalin) mimic the action of the missing neurotransmitters. To get reasonably normal functioning, the level of medication has to be calculated to make up the shortfall in the brain; too much or too little still results in dysfunction. Antidepressants are often used in the treatment of adults particularly. Again these act through their effects on the neurotransmitters including dopamine.

Often by the time medication is prescribed, significant problems typically have already arisen both in school and in the family dynamic. Behavioural therapy and other family support can attempt to mend relationships, often shattered by the time of diagnosis, and can give advice on strategies to be used at home or in school to reduce the impact that the condition has. The development of support groups for sufferers and their parents can provide great comfort to those involved.

Regrettably, ADHD often doesn't limit itself to high levels

of inattention, impulsivity and hyperactivity. With time the disruptive nature of the symptoms brings on-going negative feedback from authoritarian figures, including parents and teachers. The loss of self – esteem and self-worth is almost guaranteed and a general disinterest and loss of engagement with those around leads to further difficulties. The lack of stimulation in the brain leads to the individual seeking other sources of stimuli, often leading to difficulties with alcohol, gambling or even drug abuse. Children with ADHD are often destined to develop 'addictive' personalities.

Not surprisingly, ADHD is correlated with significant academic underachievement and difficulties with relationships and employment. People with ADHD need support, probably throughout life, to a greater or a lesser extent.

Another complication is that ADHD is seldom unaccompanied. Many sufferers have 'comorbid' conditions; conditions that occur in tandem with ADHD. Many of these can be even more debilitating than the ADHD itself. Well over half of the children diagnosed with ADHD have one or more comorbid conditions.

These comorbid conditions include learning disabilities such as dyslexia, sleeping disorders, Tourettes Syndrome, depression, conduct and oppositional defiant disorder and bipolar disorder. Conduct disorder and oppositional defiant disorder have symptoms that can be elucidated from their names. However, it can very difficult to distinguish them from each other and some of the manifestations associated with ADHD itself. The string of conditions listed have biological origins and strong genetic tendencies as with ADHD. It is not surprising to find that in the wider family of a child with ADHD a number of relatives with at least one, or a combination of, the conditions listed at the start of this paragraph.

Around about fifty percent of individuals with ADHD have a comorbid dependency on alcohol or substance abuse. Approximately fifty percent are also addicted to nicotine. Not surprisingly many suffer from multiple substance addiction. Research evidence also shows that ADHD affected individuals are more likely to experiment with tobacco, alcohol and drugs at an earlier age. Substance abuse is even more likely if another comorbid condition such as depression or anxiety also exists.

But what causes the link? Heredity is a factor in many comorbid conditions; over fifty percent of children diagnosed with Tourettes also have ADHD. But genetics is not the whole story with the strong and destructive correlation with substance abuse.

The impulsive nature of affected individuals leads to experimentation and recklessness when not controlled. Another factor is what can loosely be regarded as subconscious self-medication. Cannabis and cocaine, for example, can compensate for the missing neurotransmitters and can lead to a reduction in ADHD symptoms. It appears that these and other drugs can stimulate the release of dopamine, the very chemical that ADD suffers have in short supply. Nicotine has a basically similar effect and it is not surprising that many ADHD sufferers become addictive smokers; the one difference being that nicotine is not illegal. Most of the research emphasises the importance of beginning treatment early, certainly before the destructive patterns of addictive behaviour take root.

Learning more about ADHD as a parent of a child with the condition isn't an uplifting experience. But it does provide understanding where previously there was little and gives an insight, welcome or not, to the potential difficulties that lie in wait.

It is worth emphasising that ADHD isn't specifically a childhood condition; it extends into adulthood. It may be that many adults become more capable at managing their condition therefore the manifestations are less obvious. Perhaps as many as sixty percent of children with ADHD have symptoms that continue into adulthood and it is assumed that all adult patients also had the condition as a child. It is not surprising that it is those children most severely affected by the condition that are most likely to suffer as an adult. In adults the hyperactive element is less common but the inattentiveness and disorganisation usually exists. It can be particularly unforgiving in adults as there is often no one around to pick up the pieces and continually watch over them.

The adult condition is less studied – most research has really only taken place in the last thirty years - but the consequences are well documented. Affected individuals usually have chronic organisational and attention problems and the low self-esteem associated with children. They are more prone to suffer from addiction problems possibly because they are less likely to have parents regulating their alcohol intake or restricting their substance abuse. Depression and co-ordination problems commonly accompany the other symptoms. Uniquely adult symptoms include work-related problems and an increased risk of having an accident when driving. Not surprisingly a significant number of affected adults spend time in psychiatric institutions and / or prison.

Perhaps a little knowledge is not always a dangerous thing; without too much knowledge it was easier to hope that Andrew would soon grow out of the condition. And how much were we going to have to pay for the 14 wasted years trying to get a diagnosis?

Update: Research published in the Lancet in late 2010 provided further clarity on the genetics underpinning the condition. In a study analysing the genomes of 366 children clinically diagnosed with ADD/ADHD and comparing them to a control of 1000 children without the condition, scientists at Cardiff University confirmed that the children with ADD/ADHD were almost twice as likely to show chromosome damage (sections missing or duplicated) and that there was a significant overlap in damage with sections of chromosome 16 that are implicated in autism and schizophrenia. Further evidence that ADD has some degree of shared biological basis with the other conditions.

Chapter 7

Looking back at the most volatile mid-teenage years, events are catalogued by educational year and age. Year 12 (the GCSE year) did not show the improvement hoped for following diagnosis. Ritalin, in either its quick release or slow release forms didn't appear to be particularly effective. Of course, medicinal intervention may not have been given a real chance; missed medication or tablets taken late became the order of the day. We seemed beyond the help of other strategies including behavioural therapy and the outlook seemed bleak.

Taking the year chronologically, the first milestone was our second brush with the police. The phone call came about eight on a Friday evening. The female constable's tone was reassuring. 'Andrew is in the police station. He was getting a lift home in a car we stopped. The car was found to have drugs in it. We don't think Andrew was involved but we will ask him a few questions. Could you please come in when we do this and then he should be free to go home.' I knew where the police station was but had yet to enter its bleak doors; another first.

Andrew was in an interview room in the Custody Suite. I was taken to him and in due course we met the sergeant on duty. Andrew's details were logged and then he had to empty his pockets out. It was then that the shiny aluminium tin, a round cylinder with a screw cap lid, about five centimetres long appeared. I hadn't seen it before but it seemed of interest to the sergeant. 'Andrew, please open that for me'. It was slowly opened and thankfully proved to be empty. 'There is a God', I thought (albeit only briefly). The sergeant wasn't satisfied though and suggested that Andrew used it for storing cannabis. Following Andrew's denial he sent for the young constable who had been on the phone. The sergeant explained to me that the young constable was the station expert; 'She can sniff out cannabis even if there is none left'. As if to prove her expertise in this field she quickly confirmed to the sergeant that there had been cannabis in the tin. I was given a quick sniff – with no effect – and the canister was then removed, put in a plastic bag and labelled, no doubt to be used as evidence.

Suspicions aroused by the aluminium canister had changed the tenor; Andrew was now going to be formally interviewed by the investigating officer, an older, stern looking man who had the look of ex-army about him. I accompanied Andrew to the interview room. The tape was switched on and the official pre-amble of names and times began. I knew what was coming. I had heard it so often on TV. The interview got increasingly uncomfortable. Andrew was clearly agitated and was vehemently denying any knowledge of the drugs found in the car. I later found out that the cling-wrapped cannabis resin was found in the recess behind the back seat. I had already worked out that the police must have had an 'interest' in the car or at least one of its occupants. As if I needed it, further evidence of the kind of company Andrew was keeping. I could see where the interview was leading; Andrew was clearly 'off the wall', whether due to the stress of the occasion or the after-effects of some illegal substance I couldn't tell. When I could see that the police officer was starting to become agitated in response to Andrew's aggression I informed the officer that Andrew had ADD and that I didn't think he would get much more out of him tonight. Without hesitation, the officer stopped the interview informing the tape as to why he had terminated it unexpectedly. The atmosphere calmed almost immediately. I suspected that the officer had been through this all before; he didn't need to ask what ADD was. A few years later I was to read that the police in our area had set up a liaison group with the families of children who were diagnosed with ADD, no doubt to try to circumvent trouble before it happened. They knew the frequent outcomes for children diagnosed with this condition. Another far-seeing and good idea; but again too late for Andrew.

It was agreed that Andrew and I would return to complete the interview the following Thursday – this give me time to think and also to organise a solicitor.

The following Thursday we returned to the station and completed the process. The solicitor gave a few bits of advice and chirped in once or twice during the interview. I couldn't help think that they get their money easy. We were told that the Crown Prosecution Service would be in touch in due course should they be able to identify the presence of cannabis in the canister or Andrew's fingerprints be found to be on the cling-film that contained the cannabis resin found in the car.

In the event they were not in touch. The few months anxiously waiting for the non-existent summons didn't do much though for our mood. That was our sentence.

Andrew's school was aware of the ADD diagnosis but life still proved to be difficult. Conflict with specific teachers was an ongoing battle and significant underachievement in his GCSE subjects was on the horizon. Detentions and phone calls or letters home became the norm. The school was becoming increasingly concerned with Andrew's own progress but also the effect his impulsivity was having on the classroom dynamic – 'other pupils were being affected in this most important year'. Mornings became a nightmare; Andrew didn't want to go to school and the school increasingly didn't want him. Around January, after much soul searching and debate, Sarah and I agreed to remove him from school for at least a short period to allow things to calm down. This was precipitated by him being removed from one teacher's class and spending the periods she taught the class in isolation to diffuse the very volatile relationship with the teacher concerned. We thought it was better to act first before our hand was forced.

Were we going to educate him at home (Sarah was between jobs at this stage; she had re-entered the teaching workforce but like many mothers who gave up full-time work to have children found it difficult to get back into permanent work and tended to rotate through temporary contracts) or was there some form of alternative provision? I didn't know where to start. Thankfully Sarah was much better equipped than me to pursue the alternatives.

Eventually, she managed to find a facility that catered for children in Andrew's position – they normally had about 15 – 20 pupils on their books and there was a vacancy at this time. Interviews were arranged. A few days later the centre, specialising in providing educational support for troubled children, agreed to take Andrew and he agreed to go. The centre was loosely affiliated to a religious order, and some of the staff (volunteers?) were members of the order so had the prefix 'Brother'. Andrew was now officially classified as being educated through EOTAS (Educated other than at School). The agreement was that he would complete a number of his core GCSE subjects through the EOTAS scheme and sit the actual exams in his mainstream school.

The arrangement was quite loose – Andrew had a contract, he was expected to turn up on time and he was expected to work when at the centre. Additionally, he was expected to behave. But the small group, or even one-to-one, tuition did allow flexibility; time out periods could be taken when the pressure mounted and relationships were much more open. The Brothers weren't trying to maintain order in a class of thirty! We realised how lucky we were. These EOTAS places were like gold dust and we had found one within a couple of days from a standing start. Normally schools have great difficulty in finding places in these facilities and they have direct contact with Educational Welfare Officers and Area Board psychologists and other specialist staff.

Progress was being made. Attendance was very good and there was no resistance to making the circuitous journey to and from 'college' every day. The Brother in charge of Andrew made contact with us on a regular basis by phone and on one such call he informed us that Andrew was so motivated he was doing a number of 'in-house' courses that would lead to certification at the end of the year. He, and we, were very pleased with progress so far.

Life on the home front had settled into a white-knuckle ride. While relations were often cordial, the potential for explosions of rage was still present. The wear and tear on everyone was palpable. Neighbours must have known the difficulties we were going through – the police occasionally arrived to give us support in calming Andrew after a particularly difficult time – but this was a topic to be avoided during neighbourly chats. Much too controversial to be discussed; the vagaries of the weather was much more suitable.

Andrew's friendships at this time tended to be transient but intense. I usually drove him to his destinations – he went out most nights. He could go to a particular friend's house virtually every night for a few weeks then to someone else most nights for a similar period. Who knows what the parents of his friends made of this. This was the pattern throughout most of the year; homework was off the radar for Andrew and it was well down our list of priorities. With Andrew content to continue with his EOTAS programme he did tend to come in most evenings during the week. Weekends were a different matter. The predictable routine of staying out all night and deliberately being out of contact made life very difficult. It was the not knowing – knowing that he was almost certainly feeding his body a cocktail of alcohol and drugs yet being unable to do anything except worry.

This was particularly difficult on Sarah. I would be dispatched to look for Andrew in the early hours. I would spend hours driving round his haunts but as often as not would not make contact. There was no point in going home to report that I hadn't found him. This would add to the worry. I would drive around hoping that I came upon him or he would switch his mobile back on. If not, hopefully Sarah would be asleep when I got home.

It was around this time that we were having doubts about our ability to cope with Andrew in the house. As Sarah wilted I began to hear the dreaded 'It's him or me. We both cannot live here. You have to choose, Peter. You will need to buy me a flat if you choose him.' This was an impossible decision. How could I choose? Andrew couldn't cope on his own and would only end up deeper in trouble. While perhaps we could switch off the face to face conflict we couldn't switch off the worry like a tap; we couldn't switch off the mess. Some of Sarah's friends were promoting this 'tough love' option, but I, rightly or wrongly, concentrated on smoothing things over and where possible pre-empting trouble. Not that there was much evidence that the alternative produced positive results. While this may have been the route of the much publicised Julie Myerson, reading her narrative indicates that zero tolerance or tough love doesn't come easy either.

Our own relationship was under pressure; how could it not be? Andrew's ability to drive a wedge between us created added stress. It was difficult to know where it would all end.

Fishing provided respite for us all. It was the one activity that could keep Andrew occupied for days on end. He would leave home at sunrise and not return until well after dark. Fish in the bag or not, it was usually a positive influence. We all benefited; Andrew could benefit from a session's fishing for a few days and we knew where he was and he was happy with us knowing where he was. Fish for supper was merely a bonus. When I asked him how could he enjoy several hours sitting in the cold and rain and not even getting a bite, let alone catch a fish, his eyes would light up as he tried to explain.

He wasn't able to define it in words but I think he enjoyed the peace and quiet. No one was expecting anything from him. The absence of pressure is what he needed. He really was a kind, loving child when he had the monkey lifted from his back.

For his birthday we bought him a fly tying kit. He spent hours getting information about the best flies to use and more hours honing the skill. As summer approached and his peers were spending the evenings learning equations and developing exam technique, Andrew was sitting on the river's bank waiting for a fish to bite. To the casual onlooker, here was a teenager at one with nature.

In due course the GCSE exams arrived and Andrew took his leave from the EOTAS scheme. There was no doubt that the caring environment, the small group work, and the positive ethos did work. The staff did seem genuinely fond of Andrew; they told us on more than one occasion how proud they were of him. Andrew's lead tutor, Brother Fergal, continued to write to him for years after he left.

The GCSE results arrived in August. Andrew had obtained six good grades including grade B's in the core subjects of English, Maths and Science. He clearly was a bright child. It made me sad to reflect on what could have been.

Chapter 8

Much of the summer after GCSEs was spent in France. France had long been a favoured destination since the children were young. Long balmy weeks were spent in *Keycamp* mobiles. Although Brittany was our favourite destination, this summer we had ventured much further south to Gascony and the Dordogne.

Gascony was the first stop. The campsite nested within a large pine forest – typical of the Atlantic fringes in south west France. Although the largest campsite we had ever been on, it didn't seem like it. The spacious pitches and the woodland screening meant that you could seldom see more than a few mobiles from any one point. It was everything we could have asked for.

Andrew and Suzanne loved the campsite, as did the young Rebecca. Two key requirements were there; many potential friends and lots of activities. Much of their time was spent on the shore of the lake that dominated the local topography. All types of water – based sports were on offer. In the evenings older teenagers would meet in droves on the lake shore, listen to music and have a ball. We knew there was drinking. There was little we could do and to have tried to prevent it would have created an unnecessary confrontation. It was better to pick our battles; fight the ones we could win. He seldom appeared to show the effects of the evening's intake – either he was not taking too much or else his capacity had grown. Better not to know.

The ADD still had the potential to break the peace at any time. Confrontations could spark in a flash. We had taken the fishing rods with us. The fishing, often for hours on end, again provided respite. When he was focused on the fishing nothing else mattered. He did need support; we had to make sure everything was packed for him, that he had his phone and lunch and all the fishing extras. Organisational ability had reached an all time low.

Horse riding also was a welcome distraction for Andrew. Once he was on the pony the tasks of getting on with daily life and relationships were no longer there. Disorganisation wasn't an issue once safely in the saddle. To the fellow campers we met and got to know around the BBQ in the long balmy evenings everything must have seemed fine; we were just like any other normal family. France came and went and left a host of great memories.

GCSE results day was a day to savour. We all knew that six GCSE grades with a mixture of B and C grades was a remarkable achievement. Not particularly noteworthy in a selective school if everything else was equal; but we knew we weren't on a level playing field. Even some of the teachers saw this as a real achievement.

Not surprisingly, Andrew wanted to celebrate his results by going out to a nightclub. The perennial problems for many GCSE pupils receiving their results had been anticipated. Fake ID had been organised – it was almost a rite of passage. Like most parents we were delighted with the performance but concerned by how the night might pan out. We had other particular concerns and were not a little intrigued by the unusual position that Andrew found himself in. Who would he celebrate with? Two 'schools' had contributed to his preparation, with perhaps his few months of EOTAS being even more significant than the traditional route.

What might lie ahead in September also exercised our thoughts. The automatic return to the Sixth Form for 'A' level study for so many of his peers didn't apply to him. The academic route was not for him; certainly not at this stage of his development. I'm sure his school had also made this assumption. However, decisions on this could wait for a few more days.

In the end he chose to go out with both groups – the afternoon of the results day was spent with two or three EOTAS students; the evening, the meat of the celebrating, with some of his old school friends.

Andrew had instigated no discussion about what could come after his GCSE years. Discussion always prompted by others, didn't get too far. I suspect he didn't really have an idea what he wanted to do. Strategic thinking was way beyond his capabilities. It was left to Sarah and me to make a few suggestions. These tentative proposals tended to focus on Andrew taking a course at the local 'tech' or College of Further Education. We surmised that the more vocationally orientated ethos, coupled with the wider range of applied courses on offer, might have something that would interest him. Eventually we did persuade him to attend a tech open day where information and expertise about the full range of courses was available. With an attitude somewhere short of enthusiasm or commitment, he did enrol for a two year double AVCE in ICT and a single AVCE in Business – the equivalent of three 'A' levels we were led to believe.

At least we didn't have to worry about the stress of having to kit him out in a uniform. The 'tech uniform' was jeans and tee shirt. All we had to do was make sure he had enough of these. For Andrew, a further bonus was that classes didn't start until the end of the first week in September and you only had to attend when you had classes; none of the prison-like regimentation of school.

Life at home was OK. We had other positive things to focus on. Andrew's elder sister had also finished important exams, in her case her 'A' levels and she was going off to university. She had achieved AAB and was going to Newcastle University to study medicine. Although we were extremely proud there did seem to a little bit of irony in it all – we could only guess when her training would lead her to confront ADHD and what would her tutors make of it all? Would they see it as a real neurobiological condition or would it be pigeon-holed in the 'put it down to poor parenting' camp? We did have a lot of work to do to get Suzanne organised – boat to be booked, new clothes to be bought and the typical student flat accessories. A degree of financial planning was also required; finding her accommodation costs was going to have to be bracketed into the monthly budget.

September arrived and the course at the tech started without too much fanfare. It all seemed pretty painless. Andrew would catch the bus at eight and return around five; some evenings he would stay on a bit later with his friends. He never had any homework. 'I get it all done in my free time and most of it is coursework anyway'. Didn't surprise me, techs had that reputation. No wonder they were anathema to so many. He attended the one in Belfast and at least it had a better reputation than the local one.

After a few weeks things seemed even better for him. Fridays were now a day off. By agreement the few Friday classes had been moved to other days of the week to give everyone a four day week. Nice work if you can get it, I couldn't help thinking. Still if they could produce the goods at the end of the two years, so be it. I would wait until I cast my eye over his first report before making judgement. I was intrigued as to how he would do, if not doing something he really liked, at least doing something he didn't appear to actively dislike.

There was a definite aura of a fresh start. Although now September it was still the millennium year and the changes in educational direction of our two elder children simply reinforced this feeling of a new dawn.

Chapter 9

Trinity Park is one of those large sprawling housing estates that the middle classes love to hate. The houses are built of grey breeze block; cheap wooden cladding invariably in need of restoration or painting adorns the façades. Lawns are nothing more than small patches of grass that were probably cheaper to develop and maintain than concrete or tarmac. The whole place oozes deprivation and poverty. It seems as if all the inhabitants dress in the 'uniform' of track bottoms and tee shirt – preferable navy or black with a stripe running down the outside of the legs. Obesity appears to be obligatory as does high fecundity. Prams are more common than cars. A rich research area for the sociologist analysing all that is wrong with modern society.

It is one of those places you drive past, but not into, and scarcely gave a second glance as you bypass one of its many entrances. I was driving past it on one of those rare days when there was enough time to go home for lunch. Although not consciously looking, I knew there was something significant about the group of youths hanging around the entrance to Trinity Park. A furtive second glance confirmed all I needed to know; Andrew was in that group. What was he doing here, five miles away from his college? Now was not the time to find out. Better to plan how to handle this one.

Lunch was not the pleasurable experience I had hoped it would be. I couldn't get Andrew out of my mind. I didn't want to discuss what I had seen with Sarah. Why have everyone worried?

When Andrew came home that evening nothing seemed out of the ordinary. He was in good form and no more or less communicative than normal.

However, it was time to try to get to the bottom of his appearance in Trinity Park. 'Andrew, how did college go today?' The response was predictable. 'Fine.' I knew that he was lying. 'I thought I saw you at the entrance to Trinity Park today. What were you doing there?' The aggressive reaction confirmed that he had been there even though he denied being anywhere near the place. There was little to be gained, except more conflict, by pursuing this any further at this stage.

The next port of call would have to be his course director at college. Was this a rare day skipping classes or was it part of a sequence of absences. I dreaded to think.

It was late the next afternoon before I could track down Andrew's course director. He seemed to be in meetings according to the switchboard all morning. Perhaps a euphemism for only starting at lunch time. I didn't want to start about the attendance straight away; it might be better to try to get some feedback on overall progress first. Andrew was bright and progress was bound to be good, I thought. 'Hello, this is the course director for full time AVCE ICT students, who is that you are asking about?' 'Andrew Moore, he started in September.' 'Please wait until I get my course details'. Why couldn't he answer me straight away? Good teachers should know intuitively how their charges are doing. Why did he need to refer to his register? His response came in the measured tones of someone who spends his time fielding awkward questions. 'Andrew left us on the 20th September. He hasn't been here for the last six weeks'. He must have known from the hesitancy in my voice that this was new to me.

I didn't know what to feel. I was angry for being made a fool of – I'm sure the course director thought to himself that here was another of those parents that hasn't a clue what is going on. 'No wonder the world is in the state it is when parents don't know what their children are doing', I could imagine it all and was concerned and pissed off. What was Andrew doing all those days when he was supposed to be going to college. Hanging around the streets, but doing what? I dreaded to think. It was easy to panic. Education could provide some hope for the future. Without the stability of education it was difficult to imagine what the next few years would bring.

Even working out how to handle this made me depressed. Sarah had to be told; Andrew had to be confronted. More hassle. Drifting wasn't going to get us anywhere.

In the end it wasn't hard to get at what appeared to be the truth. Andrew said that he had no interest in the course and gradually stopped going. When he was too far behind to catch up that was the time to stop. He didn't want to tell us he had left – he thought we had had enough disappointments - so spent the days in friends' houses or hanging around the town. While it was all so predictable, the past couldn't be changed; it was important to plan ahead. But what could he do – it was now November.

Andrew accepted that phantom visits to college were no longer on. He was going to have to do something. He informed us that he was going to get a job to see him through for the rest of the academic year and think about furthering his education later.

Thankfully, he found a job fairly quickly. He was going to be taken on as casual labour in a local concrete products business. The work was bound to be heavy. Making breeze blocks and other concrete structures required hard physical effort but little in the way of initiative. It did suit him though. On occasions the other workers told him to slow down. He was working too fast and was going to burn himself out, they would say. I couldn't help thinking it was part of the ADD. Multi-tasking wasn't required here - he simply needed to programme himself for the day's task and switch his motor on and that was that.

By the time Christmas arrived he had become established within the small workforce. He was known as a fine worker and the boss thought highly of his work ethos. He fitted in well with the Poles and Lithuanians that seemed to dominate the workforce. For Christmas he bought us an ornamental 'man and barrow', a concrete mould about one metre in length and typical of those seen in many gardens. The idea was to plant a few perennials in the barrow and station it on the back patio. It definitely was a good idea although Andrew could never quite establish if he had made this particular sculpture himself.

Christmas was a good family time. Suzanne was home for her first university holidays and we had the first snow for several years. To the casual visitor things were idyllic.

It was still very cold in early January when we all had to start back to work. Andrew started back with a slight back strain; probably a consequence of heaving concrete all day long. One could only guess what the Health and Safety Executive would make of the work regime in the concrete world. 2000 seemed well before the requirement for courses in heavy lifting or for risk assessment exercises.

As the months progressed Andrew's mood deteriorated. There was no obvious reason why, but I suspected that there was a change in his drug habit or that there was something else that was worrying him. It became increasingly difficult to waken him in the morning and it was always difficult to gauge the best approach; whether the stern or soft soaping approach was likely to be more successful. His boss picked him up in the morning, even though we lived only half a mile away from the industrial plant. He was patient; he recognised in Andrew an intelligent and willing worker when he was in the mood and I suspect he realised that confrontation was not always the best way forward. On some occasions he waited for up to twenty minutes and on other occasions he drove on to work without him. On those occasions, Andrew usually did eventually make it, albeit late.

Andrew started going out most nights now. He would return late and it was always difficult to get any details of where he had been or what he had been up to. It was a never ending circle – the more he went out the more difficult it was to get him up. Communication became very truncated and we were always walking on eggs. Reason was not part of the equation.

Not surprisingly, Andrew and the concrete business parted company around mid-April. His good days were becoming less frequent and his work ethic was further hindered by the development of recurrent back pain. I was further plagued by the thought that I was negligent in letting him work in this environment where musculo-skeletal injury seemed a matter of when and not if.

Chapter 10

Yet again the fishing brought respite and on occasions it could be for a whole weekend. It was genuine comfort as his fishing friends were 'normal.' While they took alcohol and some may even have tried cannabis, they were real friends. Friends that looked after you and tried to keep you from doing something really stupid; friends that stood by you when things got really tough.

Andrew was becoming a good fisherman too; people would seek out his advice on where to fish or what type of fly to use. His peers marvelled at the 22 lb pike he caught in a local lake. It was photographed time and time again, with or without its captor. For a week it was even stored in the freezer in the garage until everyone who might want to see it had seen it. It seemed that only a physical sighting would do for some of the sceptics.

Fishing weekends really seemed to lift his mood – I suppose they were proxy scouting camps. Catching your dinner in the river and scavenging for wood to light the bonfire were all part of the fun.

Andrew had followed family tradition by joining the scouting movement. I had benefited enormously from the camaraderie that scouting provided for teenage boys and eventually became a Queen's Scout. Sleeping rough and fending for ourselves as we trained for our 'Backwoodsmans' badge was little different to the activities of a fishing weekend. While I had a long relationship with scouting and eventually put something back into the organisation by serving a few years as a scout leader, Andrew's dalliance with the organisation was all too short. While he proved to be a very enthusiastic and committed member, the discipline required proved to be too much and he had left by the time he was fifteen. The manner of his departure could be summarised by that oft-used phrase that accompanies the departure of a Premiership football manager, 'by mutual consent'.

By mid-year Andrew gave every appearance of someone who was in trouble. The pockmarked face and sunken eyes were tell-tale signs of drug and alcohol abuse. He was becoming increasingly listless around the house and he had visibly changed over the space of a few months. His behaviour oscillated between what could pass as normal and what could only be described as being totally disturbed. It was difficult to elucidate if the most discordant behaviour was caused by him being on drugs at that time or just the cumulative effect on his brain or even what role the wear and tear of having a heartless condition such as ADD played in the mix.

He could disappear for two or three days and was beginning to come under the influence of one or two very shady individuals who no doubt were complicit in supplying him with his illicit requirements; individuals you knew as soon as you saw them were up to no good.

Most people are probably unaware of the potential of the police as two-way conduits of information in keeping things under control. Good citizens understand that certain types of information should be given to the police; information concerning potential or real criminal activity. While TV viewers will be aware of police information films on drink driving, burglary and a host of other areas, fewer have experience of the police's role in passing advice at a personal level.

Not unsurprisingly, the police were aware of Andrew's activities. They certainly appeared to be interested in some of his associates. On a small number of occasions around this time we would get casual visits or calls from one of the local officers. It was often the same officer, a friendly, experienced man who looked as if he had experienced most of what life had to offer. He had a 'lived in' face. We would chat over a cup of tea or coffee about absolutely anything but we would always get round to discussing our son. As he often said he was 'on the fringes of a bad crowd'. We knew this but we did find the contact invaluable, almost supportive. They would 'continue to keep an eye on things'. He was warm and understanding. He knew that we were doing all we could to keep Andrew stable but accepted that there was little we could do. We did discuss the possibility of making contact with the mental health services again.

The police knew all about ADD – their statistics had shown that many of the youths they came in contact with had been identified as having had this condition. Being proactive and innovative, as already noted, local officers had set up a liaison group in the area that attempted to build relationships with children in the area with ADD and their families, before they got in trouble. An excellent idea but perhaps idealistic; we knew that the effect of the genes are not easily overcome. Our relationship with the police was something similar, but as before, it was probably too little and certainly too late.

Being over sixteen, Andrew was no longer within the remit of the local NHS Children's Care services – he was now officially an adult, although some years from the levels of maturity normally associated with the title. He had drifted away from using Ritalin as a medicine. While he would still get it on prescription, he and we were no longer convinced of its value in his case; again possibly too little, too late. Perhaps he hadn't given the medication a real chance; it was difficult to tell.

Before we could persuade Andrew to go down the medical path again events dictated our strategy. One particular Sunday afternoon proved to be a key pivotal point. As was normal at this time, Andrew had been out of the house since Saturday morning.

However, he did agree to be home by lunch time on Sunday in time to get ready for a visit to his grandparents. By Sunday morning tensions were rising; Andrew still agreed to go on the visit but was adamant that he would arrive 'exactly as the car was about to leave'. This wasn't really acceptable to us; we knew he would probably need to have a shower and change.

Eventually he did arrive back on time but he was clearly 'out of it'. He literally bounced around the kitchen from worktop to worktop and was barely coherent. There was no way he was going visiting in this condition but he couldn't be left either. It didn't take long for him to explode and storm out of the house ranting that he would walk the five miles back to his friends. Before he left his throwaway remark was that he had taken a handful of Ritalin tablets – we had no way of knowing whether this was true or not.

He was in no fit state to be on the public roads. I drove after him to try and persuade him to get in the car and come back as Sarah contacted the police and informed them that we had a potential overdose situation. Andrew refused to talk to me or get in the car and seemed totally impervious to the danger he was in. Veering back and forth across the road, half running half walking, as cars drove past at speed causing more that one driver to swerve or break violently. This seemed to have little effect on him; it was impossible to know how much he was aware of what was going on.

After what seemed a lifetime, the marked police car coming from the opposite direction pulled onto the hard shoulder just short of the point Andrew had reached. The officer quickly got out and asked him to get in the car. After initial remonstrating he agreed and both cars then made the short journey back to the house. As Andrew and the lead officer came in, the female driver wandered round to the back of the bungalow. A strange move I thought at the time but it later transpired this was a move to prevent him escaping out a back window or door. The police were not heavy handed but quietly succeeded in calming him down. They did this with some effect; they were clearly experienced and quickly accepted that they were dealing with something slightly out of the ordinary.

Eventually they persuaded Andrew to go to the A&E department at the local hospital where he could be checked over. While it was clear he had taken some substances they had no way of knowing just how much. Andrew now denied having taken 'a handful of Ritalin' but no one could be sure. Certainly from the state he was in more corroborating evidence was required above and beyond what he was saying.

It was agreed that he would travel with me and the police would follow close behind. They advised that they would alert the hospital in advance about what they could be faced with.

The police were taking no chances. The officer quietly said to me as we left. 'one wrong move out of him and we will have him sectioned. I'm not sure if that's not what he needs anyway'. On that positive note we headed down the motorway to our destination.

In the casualty department we were seen immediately. The advance warning had obviously reached the right people. Eventually it was agreed that Andrew had not taken a significant overdose and the level of drugs in his system were not going to cause him immediate harm. There were, of course, warnings about the long-term effects of substance abuse and the suggestion that a visit to the GP could trigger some follow-up psychiatric support if required. It all seemed so easy.

The rest of the summer was a bit more stable. He seemed to gradually wean himself away from the crowd he had been associating with in recent months and make more contact with his older friends. Tensions at home were reduced; possibly because he was less under the influence of drugs. He still appeared to be using them but at a much reduced level. Perhaps we could get round to talking about what the future might bring.

Chapter 11

Like many boys of his age, reading the papers was not high on Andrew's agenda. Reading, when it happened, constituted a quick flick through a 'red top'. Pictures tended to be more relevant than prose. The immediacy of the information was what was needed.

Consequently, it was all the more surprising when he spotted an advert that interested him in a local daily. The advert was offering two competitive Modern Apprenticeship positions in Roofing and Tiling with a multinational concern that had a local plant only a few miles away from our village. Application was by application form and subsequent interview.

We had long ago realised that the academic route was unlikely but a genuine interest in any career path was a very positive move. Forms were sent for, completed and in due course an interview was arranged.

The interview went very well, according to Andrew, and he was proved correct when an offer of a place came a few weeks later. Apparently he had impressed the interviewers with his understanding of the format of a Modern Apprenticeship and had convinced them of his ability to cope equally with both the trade and theoretical elements of the position. Having a Grammar School background and a good GCSE profile probably helped show that he could easily cope with the academic element that many apprentices struggle with.

The apprenticeship would last between 3-4 years and he was guaranteed employment with the multinational for the duration of the course. Andrew, as we all were, was delighted with the outcome of his application and looked forward to the start of the course with much enthusiasm. Like the older traditional apprenticeships it had a sandwich element – part taught in the local construction industry training centre and part work placement with a squad of roofers. It did seem that this just might be more than yet another false dawn.

Early weeks were very positive for all concerned. It didn't take long for the technical jargon of the roofer to become part of the everyday vocabulary. He made some good friends and his senior colleagues were genuinely caring. The company concerned was investing heavily in his training and were obviously determined to get a sound return for their investments.

A regular income and the independence it gave was a further bonus. Andrew had now become a fully paid up member of the household.

For a couple of years things progressed relatively smoothly with just the occasional hiccup. He became more reliable and had a good, and expanding range, of solid friends and workmates. Assessments were passed with relative ease and progress on placement was going well. Time-keeping was not a problem, as part of the contract was that the company would provide transport to and from work. If it was a study day it was transport by taxi, if on placement, the squad supervisor did the lifting.

Things on the home front were pretty good too. Although prone to the blips typical of many late teenager boys such as a tendency to drink too much on occasions, he was more considerate than before. Genuine empathy was a bridge too far but certainly things were better.

The standard rituals of the developing teenager including learning to drive were faced and eventually overcome. The impulsive nature, now totally ingrained in Andrew's character, cost him dearly the first two times the driving test was taken, but success eventually followed.

In his third year as an apprentice he made contact again with some of his old school friends that he had not been in touch with for a few years. The epicentre of his socialisation gradually moved towards the university area of Belfast. Although enjoying his work, both the flexibility of student life and the buzz of its social life made him envious on occasions. There were the occasional regrets that he was not following the path of so many of his peers. As a compromise he was contemplating moving into a flat in Belfast; a flat that would be part of the 'social scene'.

He did discuss this in detail with us. There were obvious pros and cons. So much would depend on who he chose to live with; he still needed a lot of support. There was little doubt that we would have to give him support as well, probably financially as well as socially. The move would make him more independent, give him more freedom at a time when most twenty year olds were experiencing independent living away from home. He seemed much more stable now. Certainly always the 'life and soul of the party,' but to the casual onlooker no different to any other immature young man. The worst effects of ADD seemed a distant memory.

Around November time he moved out. He had done the research himself and was moving into a house deep in the city's student land. I agreed to act as guarantor and helped him buy some essentials before he moved in. The house was fully furnished and he was moving in with another apprentice in the building trade. We knew the individual concerned; he wouldn't have been our first choice as a housemate for Andrew but we thought it would be all right. There was room for one more and the intention was that in due course they would find another lodger to help with the rent.

He seemed to adapt fairly well to his new life. Certainly he found it very hard to manage his money. The day to day expenses could be managed but rent week was always a difficult time. He still had a lot to learn; there were too many fast food meals each sapping away at his meagre resources. There was some cooking done and he was a good and an enthusiastic cook. He did have a washing machine in the house but the more delicate items were brought home to be done. It didn't take long for the house to become a party house. We were casually invited for a meal but I suspect the house itself had degenerated into the worst kind of student flat before too long. There were too many stories of having to get carpets cleaned for that not to be the case.

His relocation did work well from a work perspective. Now in his third year as an apprentice there was relatively little in the way of college based theory. Most of his time was spent on placement. Assessment tended to take place through visits on site. Progress was being made.

Chapter 12

Andrew's visits home had become relatively infrequent and he began looking more unkempt and jaded. He was also beginning to find it more difficult to manage financially. After thirteen months of independent living he mentioned that he was considering returning home. He asked if that would be possible. It was difficult to say why but I couldn't help thinking that something was wrong; I just had that feeling of dread in my gut.

My fears were realised when he came for lunch the following Sunday. He looked dreadful and his pallor was ashen grey. The story was blurted out after lunch. He had been dependent on cannabis for some time and had recently started using cocaine. We knew he had used cannabis in the past but had thought (hoped!) that he was largely off it; the cocaine was a real shock. He said he needed help and thought that his brain had been affected. He was going to seek treatment.

Still shell-shocked from what we heard things rapidly went downhill. 'I'm in court next Thursday on drugs charges'. I could only reflex, 'What charges?' Caught in possession of drugs. 'Where are you in court?' 'Belfast' was his answer. 'How in the name of God did this all happen?' 'We were having a three day party and the police raided the house – six of us got arrested.'

How does a parent react to this? Sarah was surprisingly calm at the moment – was it because she was too dazed to take it in? My mind was in turmoil. I couldn't decide what to do next. Who needed to be informed? Did he have a solicitor?

All the defendants appeared in court on Thursday as required.

The charges were withdrawn but this was only a technicality. They were withdrawn so that the Crown Prosecution Service could review the evidence and formally press charges in due course based on a considered review of the available information. I had little doubt that this was only a temporary reprieve. It was pretty obvious that the evidence was there for at least some charges to stick. The whole thing was a sorry mess. Andrew had been interviewed in the station following his arrest and although barely fit to speak, and without a solicitor in attendance, had admitted his guilt to possessing cannabis and cocaine. It was difficult to see the way forward. But he is our son and we would do what we could to help him – this was about all we could agree to at this stage. Nothing had prepared us for the journey we were about to embark on. We couldn't help thinking what we had done to deserve this.

We had to fight the war on a number of fronts. The legal end would surface in due course. The addiction had to be faced first. Andrew admitted that he knew he was getting into trouble on that front. He didn't know whether he was just dependent or an addict. What is the difference? Is there a difference? Perhaps just in the context it is used in the press and on TV. He agreed to make an appointment with his GP. That was an obvious place to start.

It was also a time of reflection for ourselves. Why had we not seen this coming? We knew that while many of the symptoms of ADD could be controlled in time he still had the underlying condition. His personality was no less addictive than it ever had been. The Internet and other sources from which we gleaned our information on ADD had warned about the addictive personalities many sufferers developed; I remembered that they also warned that a high percentage of people with the condition touched base with the criminal justice system. It looked as if we were going to do more than touch base with it.

Andrew's increasing engagement with substance abuse was affecting more than his legal standing and his health. He eventually informed us that he was in a bit of trouble at work. His attendance had started to slip and he was due to make a personal appearance in front of his employers to account for his recent absences and apparently, his changing attitude to work. This was precipitated by a second written warning.

The visit to the GP was a start – unlike similar visits in earlier years Andrew attended unaccompanied. He liked the long-term locum he was placed with. We knew we weren't going to get far if there wasn't trust between the two from the beginning. Andrew was honest and open and admitted that he was dependent on cannabis and risked getting hooked on cocaine as well. He was prescribed medication which was to help him break his dependency. We had very open and frank conversations in the weeks following his attempt to break his habit. He admitted that he was finding it very hard to stay off the cannabis. He couldn't sleep and he did have the occasional relapse. We also knew that to have any hope of success with his treatment he had to live at home. Living at home also meant that we could make sure that he got to work on time. After living away from home for a time I knew that his moving back in would also bring its own stresses in time. We had got used to the peace.

Eventually things improved and he was starting to get positive feedback from his employers; they could see that he was trying to turn himself around.

Within a few months it became apparent that he was to all intents and purposes drug free. For most of the time we also knew who he was with. All we had to do now was to wait for the due course of the law to take its course. It was already four months since the original court appearance. How much longer would we have to wait?

Chapter 13

2007 started well. Andrew's apprenticeship was coming to an end and he was to get a significant pay rise. He was still attending the GP on occasions and his progress was being closely monitored. Month after month passed and all was going well apart from the dark cloud that hung over everyone's head.

He graduated in the middle of the year and a ceremony to mark the completion of the apprenticeship was held in the company offices. He was now in a steady relationship and we discussed the possibility of him moving into a house with his girlfriend. She was very supportive of him and had the strength of character to help keep him on the rails. She was good for him – giving him focus and he was maturing by the day. 2007 drifted on and on. The court case lurked in the background but it was something we seldom talked about.

By the end of the year he was well established in his new life, and home, and joined the family for Christmas dinner; it was just like old times.

2008 also started well. Sarah was now working full time again after a break of a few years and life had settled into a routine. In January we booked an Easter holiday in France. It was good to be looking forward to positive experiences. We knew that for the first time in years we could go on a continental holiday without constantly worrying how Andrew would get on without us. We knew he would be OK – someone else was now carrying much of the daily burden. Things were going so well for him that he and his girlfriend were able to book a holiday in Bulgaria for May time, only a few weeks after we would be home from France. Before breaking up for Easter we went out for a family meal. Andrew and his girlfriend came along too. We were just like any other family.

Easter in France was particularly cold. We had to light the log fire most days but it was very restful nonetheless. Work had been very busy for both of us and we were in need of the rest. While not having the opportunity to sit out in the sun, the hill walking and the evening meals out were especially memorable. Walking across the roof of Brittany along the ancient Pre-Cambrian heather-shrouded schists was light years from daily drudgery. France was good for the soul.

The journey home on the cruise-liner quality Roscoff-Cork ferry added to the experience. It was a great way to finish the holiday. Monday morning and work would come all too soon. Andrew texted to say that he would call to see us in the middle of the next week; he was keen to hear how the holiday had gone. What's more, he had a couple of trout in the freezer for us.

Work on Monday was a shock to the system. The first day back is always tough. Andrew called on the Tuesday night and we had a good chat about the holiday. Just before he left he said that his solicitor had been in touch. The original charges had been preferred and he was due in court in a couple of weeks. We knew it had to come but it was still a shock. After all it was nearly eighteen months since the whole chain of events had started. That is nearly a sentence in itself. I knew it was going to be a difficult few months. We had no idea how it was going to end. A custodial sentence and all that that would bring was a real possibility. Things were going to move fast and at this stage we hadn't even told his young sister. She knew he was a bit of a loose cannon, and one of the lads, but had been too young to remember the very difficult early years. Court appearances and sentences were well beyond her experience of life.

It may have been coincidental, but Sarah's mood dipped very

significantly at this time. For her, it had very much been a case of out of sight out of mind. I genuinely think that she thought the summons would never appear - a gap of eighteen months did little to disabuse her of this comfortable outlook. Being prone to infrequent bouts of depression she knew the warning signs. She also knew it was something she couldn't ignore. She had to arrange an appointment with her GP without delay.

Anti-depressant tablets were prescribed immediately but he warned that it would take time for these to have maximum effect.

The court appearance came and went. Andrew had to appear but it was little more than formally preferring charges and confirmation of name and other details. A further hearing was organised for late April. The case was being held in the Crown Court – this was the fate of cases involving Class A drugs. This indicated that a jury would be involved and also that if convicted, sentences were likely to be more severe. Knowing that the case was to be in the Crown Court was not information to calm the nerves.

The April hearing was also a formality. The case was planned for June and the defendants were informed that they would hear the date of their trial in due course but that it looked like being mid-June, just before the summer recess. He had little in the way of defence against possession of cannabis or cocaine and possession of cocaine was a serious enough charge.

Eventually the date of the June appearance was confirmed. However, Andrew's barrister was aware that there was a lot of outstanding paperwork still to be completed. He thought that the trial couldn't proceed at that time; a postponement to after summer was likely. This proved to be the case. A quick phone call confirmed that the trial was put back until the new session. It would probably take place in September or October. The worry could be switched off for a few months. It was easier for me to do this than Sarah; she was starting to fall apart.

Chapter 14

Depression is one of those medical conditions that affects more than the depressed. It is impossible to live with someone depressed and totally escape its all-embracing tentacles. While June postponed legal difficulties it didn't have the same effect on Sarah's decline. Medication was changed and referral was made to a psychiatrist. Part of the intervention involved twice weekly visits from a Community Support Nurse (CPN) who would provide support in the home setting.

Sarah somehow remained at work through June. It was a struggle but it did have its benefits. It provided a focus on other things and a different environment. However, we were all glad when the end of June was reached and the school holidays arrived.

While depression can affect people in different ways; the very low mood, lack of self-esteem and self-worth seem to be common traits. The risk of self-harm or worse can vary. In the current medical climate, more emphasis is given to the patient's own perception of their condition – the one size fits all approach has been confined to the past. In early July, Sarah's condition continued to deteriorate and medical intervention was becoming more frequent although it was quite clear there was no magic bullet; the condition would have to run its course.

The advice was that if a major crisis should present, and the community psychiatric nurse or Sarah's psychiatrist were unavailable, the psychiatric unit in the local hospital should be contacted for advice. In the end we had a crisis and did need to contact the hospital on a Sunday afternoon in late July. The advice was that Sarah should come in for assessment.

We arrived at the hospital; ten minutes drive away, not knowing if she was going to be admitted or not. They would assess her as soon as the duty psychiatrist could arrive – this was likely to take about an hour; she was currently carrying out an assessment at a sister hospital. About ninety minutes later she arrived and the assessment began. I was seen first, presumably to gain some background information. The options were outlined to me; an assessment followed by a further urgent referral to her psychiatrist; voluntary admittance; or admittance under the Mental Health Act. The psychiatrist added that she would make the recommendation as to whether an inpatient stay was necessary but that I could influence the decision as to whether the admittance was voluntary or not.

In due course it was agreed that there would be a voluntary admittance. The psychiatrist couldn't be sure but she thought a few days might do the trick. We had come prepared so I was despatched to the car to get the bags. The psychiatric ward provided plenty of opportunities for black humour. The locked doors and windows and secure reception centre underlined the difficulties that could exist within the building. The checking of all personal contents and the removal of any objects that could be considered dangerous all added to the surreal atmosphere. Some of the patients were clearly very ill. I did think that while this environment could keep people safe it was difficult to see how it could make people better.

The only thing I could do was to visit as often as I could and provide support where possible. The first two or three days were very difficult. A difficulty reinforced by the fact that a skeleton staff rota operated at weekends – restorative work could only begin at the start of the typical working week.

The first few days had many bouts of tears. Frustration with the system, low spirits and a sense of shame all played their part. The difference between the public perceptions of physical and mental illness became all too apparent. After a couple of days Sarah accepted that she was in the right place and a few days with others carrying the burden would help. She needed rest, physical and mental, as much as anything.

By the middle of the week I knew things were getting better. Visits didn't begin with tears and an account of the deficiencies of the institution or staff. They started with stories about fellow patients; the patient who had gone off on a tantrum or the one who had been confined to his room for verbally abusing staff or whatever. By this stage the medical intervention appeared more consistent. There were the daily consultations with the psychiatrist or other member of staff. Relationships and trust were beginning to become established. Sarah had also identified those patients that she would benefit from talking to. Some could lift her spirits as effectively as others could dampen them – she had recovered enough to know that it was important to avoid the latter.

There were new difficulties on other fronts by now. Andrew and his girlfriend had separated. To me this was out of the blue. He was returning home to live. I didn't have a problem with this and the period of time living as a couple had brought further much-needed maturation. This could be an untimely blow for Sarah; now was not the time to tell her.

By the Thursday things were much better and Sarah had been told that she would probably get out sometime over the weekend. She was quite happy with this; she knew she had benefited from admission and was all too aware that some of her fellow patients were in for a much longer haul; she could see that there might be an end in sight; that her outlook mightn't always be bleak.

She was getting out on the Friday. This worked well. We were going to go away to Donegal for the weekend. Another break from routine and the spoiling that a hotel stay would bring would all help. The medical staff thought this was a great idea.

Andrew was at work as normal on the Friday. He and his colleagues were informed that there would be an emergency meeting at the company offices the following Monday week. There would be a follow-up letter to confirm arrangements, and no, the supervisor could not elaborate on what the meeting was about. Just something else to keep the pot boiling, and something else to keep from Sarah, at least for now.

Friday was one of the few sun-drenched days of the entire summer. Entering the psychiatric unit had become routine. I knew which buzzers and buttons to press and how long I could expect to wait before gaining entry. There were CCTV cameras everywhere; to the uninitiated it was probably as difficult to gain entry as to get out.

There were a few goodbyes to be said before Sarah was ready to leave; a week in there probably provided as much life experience as a few months do for most people. It still all seemed surreal to me; maybe that's what kept me sane.

Donegal proved to be a real oasis in our particular desert. The weather remained blissful throughout the weekend and west Donegal had its usual abundance of good food, good Guinness and exhilarating walks along deserted sandy beaches.

Sarah was still very fragile but the weekend was a healing experience. She had to be selective about what she could do and she spent more time in bed than is normal for such excursions but the setting or timing could scarcely have been better. Weekends like that could almost be part of the NHS!

Sunday evening came all too soon and the long drive home began. She dozed in the car and I had plenty of time to mull over some of the issues that lay ahead. It was a pity I couldn't leave all our problems on a Donegal sandy beach.

Chapter 15

CPN visits frequented the following week. I had to explain to Sarah that Andrew and his girlfriend had split up and he was now living at home for the interim.

Andrew was at work as normal but the hastily organised meeting was beginning to fuel speculation. It was no secret that construction work was slowing at a rapid pace in line with the slow down in the availability of house mortgages. The 'credit crunch' was affecting the economy in general, but the building trade was certainly taking early hits. There was a lot of talk that redundancies were in the offing.

Andrew and I debated his position. He weighed up where he stood in relation to his peers should a number of redundancies be announced. He was an excellent worker but was clearly carrying 'baggage'. We could do little else except speculate; we could do nothing until we knew numbers.

Andrew left early for his meeting on Monday morning. They had all predicted correctly. The roofing squad was going to be reduced by three as part of an initial series of cuts. It was likely that more would follow. The managers explained that an objective set of criteria were going to be used, including length of service, management experience, qualifications and skills portfolio. The workers concerned would be informed the following Monday. This was to allow time for the criteria to be effected and discussions with the unions.

Andrew planned to go fishing on the Saturday. It would be a welcome distraction for everyone. We hadn't even considered what we would do if he was made redundant. He would have to live at home now. As a diversion Suzanne was coming home for the weekend. Now a fully qualified doctor she had the maturity to realise when support was needed. She was a great support to her mother, frequently discussing her condition and recounting examples that she had met in the wards. She could also be an emotional pillar when circumstances dictated, and they dictated now.

Dinner on Saturday night was fresh trout.

Suzanne flew back on Sunday night, catching the last plane. She usually hated that flight as it was often packed with students heading back to university; however, there were no such problems in late July.

Andrew got an unexpected text from his supervisor on Sunday night. It was not good news. While he would hear officially on Monday morning, he was told that he was going to be one of the roofers made redundant. He took it extremely well; perhaps he had anticipated that he was going to one of the unlucky ones. Most of the other roofers had more experience. Using the 'last in first out' rule, he was always going to lose out. His only hope had been that he was widely regarded as one of the best roofers, and certainly one who could use his initiative.

My hand was forced. I had to tell Sarah now. I had not up to now as I calculated that there was no point in creating unnecessary worry until there was something real to worry about.

The official letter was handed out at work on Monday morning. It was a difficult time for all concerned; some employees getting redundancy notices on site and others escaping the cuts, at least for now. I could only imagine that it was worse for the roofer who was the only breadwinner in his family and had to go home to a wife and two young children.

The redundancy letters did provide a lot of the missing detail. Work would continue for another two weeks for those affected and a very generous redundancy package, well above the statutory minimum, was being paid to the staff concerned.

Andrew did continue working for the next two weeks; things were probably a bit more casual than before but the fact that he continued to go was further evidence of his increasing maturity. The company careers service provided a couple of guidance interviews but there were not too many opportunities likely to be available for redundant roofers in the increasingly gloomy economic climate.

Suzanne proved to be particularly influential at this time. We were at a loss of what to do next but she began sewing the seeds to Andrew of what he should do next. A once damaged relationship was proving to be particularly robust just when it was most needed.

Andrew had little decision making to do. Suzanne had made the decisions for him and simply fed him the right lines at the right times. The plan was for Andrew to move over to Newcastle for a few months and take a chance on finding work there. He was going to stay with Suzanne initially and she would organise a flat for him. All he had to do was find work.

To make his journey to Newcastle easier, Suzanne travelled home again for a few days holidays and then travelled back with him again on the same flight. She had been working hard behind the scenes; Andrew was to stay with her for a week and then move into a house that a number of her medical colleagues had rented.

He took little time settling in. On his first afternoon in Newcastle he was pounding the streets in search of employment. Before he left home he had updated his CV and photocopied his qualifications. Armed with multiple copies he was equipped for making Newcastle aware of what he had to offer. When helping him update his CV it was surprising to note just how well qualified he was when all his qualifications were listed together. Truncated education or not, he had amassed an impressive CV.

It took a couple of weeks, and no little financial support, but eventually he did find employment. He had unrealistic hopes of finding work as a roofer but was willing to settle for anything, within reason, that would bring in a wage. The Job Centre had found a position for him. He had the opportunity to start as a baker in a large superstore the following Monday. The contract was for three months to cover the busy pre-Christmas period but there was the possibility of an extension depending on trading conditions.

Two days training was given but the baking was generally mechanised and formulaic. He had the initiative and intelligence to make a success of it. I was glad he had found work relatively quickly; I knew he would get despondent if he had to wait too long.

Things were looking up. Feeling much more positive about himself he joined the local gym. He tried to attend every day and on occasions was in the gym before work. This was another good sign – he hadn't trained as hard since he was in the rugby team in junior school. There were few opportunities to get homesick. Suzanne made sure he was well entertained in those first few weeks before he had a chance to make his own friends. Things were as good as they had been for some time.

Chapter 16

By October 2008 Sarah was making incremental progress. The CPN still attended on a weekly basis; she was well enough informed to know that there was going to be a crisis ahead. Medication was still doled out on a regular basis but at last it looked as if it might be working.

I was in the middle of a busy period of work and was stretched to the limit doing my best to support Sarah. She was also getting good support from her close colleagues at work and through friends on the Internet. On-going news from both children in Newcastle was good.

I was used to taking phone calls through the working day. Some came through the switchboard but other colleagues would ring me direct on my mobile – saving time they would claim. Another call on my mobile seemed just that; someone else requiring something to be done immediately. This one was different. The name on the screen was not a colleague but Andrew's solicitor. I didn't need to think. I knew what this was about. It looked as if the waiting was over.

'Hi Peter, sorry to ring you at work, but I have managed to lose Andrew's number. D-Day is next week, on the Thursday. Is he still in Newcastle? It is crucial that he is back for 10.00am on the Thursday. Can I leave it to you to get him home? I'm meeting with the barrister later this morning to see what more we can do. Still think it's in the lap of the Gods'. Some God I thought.

It's hard to get back to work after a phone call like this. More decisions had to be made. Do I tell Sarah? In the end I didn't – best to keep the worrying to the absolute minimum. There was little I could do for the rest of the day, except relay the information I had received on to Andrew. I could hear the tone in his voice change as I spoke to him. Even doing this was hell. Perhaps even he had managed to put it all out of his mind.

The rest would have to wait for the evening. When I got home, and was sure Sarah was resting on the top of the bed I decided to book his flights. Better to do it myself. If I left it to him he might cut things too fine. Flights are delayed – it couldn't be left to chance. There was nothing for it. I was going to book him on the last flight on the Wednesday night – the night before.

In the end he was happy with this. He was able to take the Thursday off and work another day in lieu. The flight back was booked for the Thursday evening so he didn't miss any time at work and saved him having to go through a whole rigmarole with his boss. It was difficult to talk to him. It was obvious he was very worried. Why had it all taken so long – he wasn't the same person that he was nearly two years ago?

In the end I told Sarah on the Tuesday. She took it well. Perhaps, she had been through so much that little else was going to have an effect.

The flight was on time. He got through in quick time; no hold baggage this time. I could provide him with the suit and accessories. We had discussed the desirability of going with him to court. Sarah wasn't really fit so it was always assumed that I would go. Andrew was clear on this. We were not going. He didn't want any of his family present. I didn't argue. I was dreading going but would have if he had wanted.

When he headed off the next morning we had arrangements in place. As soon as anything was happening he was to text or ring me. It was a long day. An early text confirmed nothing official was happening until after lunch. The morning involved barristers in negotiation. The real text came in about four. There was a provisional agreement. Andrew was to plead guilty to the two possession charges. At least this avoided what we all dreaded, a trial in front of a jury. We were not out of the woods yet but a custodial sentence, while still possible, was much less likely. Like so many texts before it I set down the mobile with my heart pounding and the beads of sweat palpable on my forehead.

He was to return to court in a month's time for sentencing. Before that he would have to return back home for a meeting with a probation officer.

Everyone was in good form on the journey to the airport. When Sarah next met her CPN, even she seemed relieved as events of that Thursday were replayed. She knew how much events carried out in a Belfast courtroom were influencing the recovery of her patient.

There was a lot to be done over the next few weeks. References had to be updated or organised. I agreed to ask a family friend to produce a character reference. Andrew had already organised a reference from his former employers. It was pleasing to read this one. They went to a lot of effort and clearly Andrew had made good progress since the dark days of two years ago.

Chapter 17

The days rolled on and I knew a part of the jig-saw was missing. The probation office hadn't been in touch. This was not optional. A pre-sentence probation report was required. I knew enough, far too much for my own good, about the justice system and I knew that probation reports could carry a lot of weight.

Just as I was beginning to get concerned I got another phone call. It was from the probation office. They were trying to get in touch with Andrew but had got my number from the solicitor. I could guess what had happened. They had sent the letter outlining details of Andrew's interview with them to his former address in Belfast – the address that he had been arrested at. We organised a meeting for Andrew for the following Monday – three days before sentencing. It was going to be rushed but it was the best we could do under the circumstances. A confirmation letter would be in the post that afternoon.

An hour or so later, Andrew's solicitor was in touch. He had given the probation office my number and he wanted to know when the interview was arranged for. He had something else he wanted to slot in – a follow-up interview with the forensic psychiatrist Andrew had seen during the summer. We managed to organise this meeting for the Monday as well. Monday was going to be busy but at least I was able to organise suitable flights without too much difficulty. *Easyjet* were going to think Andrew was a business traveller. To and from Newcastle twice in the one week was hardly leisure travelling. He probably qualified for some sort of frequent flyer discount. One thing struck me as I reflected on this. Was I being over optimistic in booking a return flight back to Newcastle on the Thursday evening? What if things didn't go as well as hoped?

Andrew's travelling back and forth was proving expensive. I had to cover this; it was well beyond what he could afford. Nonetheless, it was not an insignificant sum. This just added stress to an already difficult time.

I rehearsed him over the route to the probation office. It was straightforward enough but there was no room for error. He was going on his own to this but I was to accompany him to see the forensic psychologist. I had been with him the last time; another stomach churning event. He was over an hour with the probation officer. This was to be expected. Sometimes they carried out two interviews – one in their offices and one in the home of the individual concerned. I assume this helps them form a picture of the level of support available. One interview would have to suffice on this occasion.

I met Andrew in Belfast after his probation interview. We just had time for some lunch before going to see Dr Carol Johnston.

Dr Johnston was reviewing her notes from the previous meeting as we arrived. Her offices were in the rich part of town. No doubt her fees were enormous. The format was going to be the same as before – a session with Andrew and then a short spell with me at the end. The only difference this time was that it would be much shorter – it was only to fine-tune her final report. She intended to finish it that night and send it to the solicitor by courier in the morning.

She spent about half an hour with him. She told me that she was going to recommend that he should attend a rehabilitation programme. He had told her again that he still had the occasional relapse; fewer than before, but relapses nonetheless. She still thought that he would need support to get fully off drugs. She had seen it all before. She was very experienced with these cases. Andrew's case was all too typical. A late diagnosis of ADD, or similar, was a common thread running through many of her cases. When we left she wished us well, again reminding me of her earlier comment that she would recommend that a non-custodial sentence was what was required.

After dropping Andrew at the airport I had time to nip back into work to at least clear my desk. I had no sooner opened the door when my mobile went again. This time it was the probation officer that had interviewed Andrew that morning. She just wanted to clarify a few issues that had come up for discussion during the meeting that morning. The addictive nature of Andrew's personality had obviously been a topic of conversation, I assume instigated and driven by her. Clarification was sought on his patterns of drinking and just how much I knew about his drug taking. The probation officer sounded reasonably sympathetic. There was little to suggest that her report would be too damning.

Just a few more days to go and the waiting would at last be over.

Chapter 18

As before, Andrew flew in the evening before the court appearance. I drove him there in good time the next morning. As we had agreed, I was not attending. I was going to spend the time in Belfast, close at hand if necessary. I had arranged to take the day off work; I kept my boss up to speed but how much could those not directly affected really understand? Andrew was to contact me on the mobile as soon as he had any news.

Then it came. The familiar bleep of the phone started just as the sounds of the first Christmas song of the year drifted out of the shopping arcade just in front of me.

It turned out to be a text message and not a call, "18 months probation, I'll see you in a few minutes, I'm just talking to our solicitor."

It was better than we could have hoped for. This was beyond our wildest dreams two years ago, almost exactly to the day when this all kicked off. I couldn't have felt happier.

Apparently his barrister had been excellent, backed up by very positive character and work references. The probation report and the report from the forensic psychiatrist all played their part too.

I rang our solicitor later and congratulated him on a job well done. He said that it had been clear from early in the proceedings that day that a custodial sentence was unlikely. Apparently, the judge had a bit of fun at Andrew's expense. When his barrister stated that he had come back from employment in England to attend the day's proceedings the judge quipped 'Did Mr Moore go so far as to get a return ticket? Taking a bit of a chance wasn't he?' Those experienced in legal circles, and certainly those with a good knowledge of the judge concerned, knew that it would work out all right.

Yet another trip to the airport. This time we had time to call and meet Sarah at home. She had gone to work as normal that day. She thought it was the best thing to stop her dwelling on the day's events. In the end she was calm and relaxed. Perhaps, she had done all her worrying. Her closest friends knew the significance of the day and did their best to keep her occupied.

For once I remained at the airport and watched the plane take off. You could still hear its engines as it disappeared into the darkness. The sound was almost therapeutic. How different it could have been.

I knew that I would probably have a bottle of wine that evening to celebrate if that is the right word. I knew Sarah would too and could only assume that Andrew would as well. A great weight had been lifted but we had been through too much not to know that there would be many more ups and downs ahead. Whether through the genes of ADD or through drug abuse, or more likely a combination of both, Andrew was not going to always find life straight-forward; of this I had little doubt. But that could wait for another day - it was time to enjoy the present. I was already picturing the bottle of 1990 Bordeaux, stored safely in an old fridge in the garage that would help me drift from reality in a few hours time.

Chapter 19

We had a few good weeks following the end of the court saga before Andrew's contract at the bakery finished. This was life as it should be. He, and we, had hoped that it would be continued for a longer period but he was told just before Christmas that all the temporary staff were going to be laid off when their contracts expired on Christmas Eve. Andrew had been involved in baking croissants and other similar items. The company was expecting a sharp fall off in sales of such almost – luxury products in the predicted post-Christmas slump.

He was happy enough. Most of friends were still this side of the Irish Sea and he still had some of his redundancy money. He came back to stay with us; there was really no other option. His room was still there for him and it seemed the best way to help him get back on his feet. And he was in great form; a weight had been lifted off his shoulders. There was no reason why returning home should be a problem. Meeting Andrew at the airport on Christmas Eve was a more enjoyable experience than his other arrivals earlier in the year. The Christmas holiday was good. Suzanne had managed to get the immediate holiday period off work and we were all together as a family again, albeit for only a few days before she had to return to work again. It was easy to think of the early Christmases twenty or more years ago when Christmas was a time of real joy in the home; that expectant holiday buzz was in the air.

It was also easy to think of the Christmases fifteen years ago or so when ADD became more of an issue – of course we didn't know that it was ADD at the time. One Christmas in particular stands out and Andrew must have been about nine or ten. He had always been a great *Lego* fan; perhaps he was always destined to work in the building trade. This was around the time of *Lego Technic*. Lego had become mechanised in a similar way to *Meccano* that had become mechanised years earlier. Perhaps this was an attempt to keep their market; boys approaching double figures needed something more exciting than the basic building blocks.

As things happened, Andrew got two models for Christmas, one from us (Santa) and one from an uncle. They were models of a car and a truck and both had complex battery operated moving parts – this was the *technic* part. Andrew insisted on opening both and attempting to build both on the same day. There were bits of *Lego* all over the place and we had to work hard to stop the two models getting mixed up, made all the harder by the fact that they were both in the yellow blocks that many of the *technic* models were made from. They were too complex to be rushed and in the end neither was completed on Christmas Day. I knew this was not normal; most children would have been happy to complete one on one day and leave the second model for later. In subsequent years, perhaps subconsciously, we organised presents for Andrew that required little building or had them built for him in advance. We had learned our lesson; impulsivity even influenced our present buying.

Following the Christmas holidays everything was fine for a couple of months then around Easter time things began to slip, imperceptibly at first, but nonetheless very noticeably after a period of time. Andrew had become increasingly disillusioned about his job prospects and he still had the occasional hang up about his significant former relationship. Perhaps the biggest problem was that his sleep patterns were all over the place. He couldn't sleep at night and he couldn't stay awake during the day. He made an appointment to see his GP; regrettably the locum with whom he had built a positive and beneficial relationship in the past had moved on. However, he was confident he could relate to one of the regulars that he had had dealings with in the past. He didn't need to articulate what we already knew from past experience; the building of trust between medic and patient is critical in attempting to address issues of the mind.

Sleeping tablets and anti-depressants were prescribed. The dosage was fairly high. The sleeping continued to be erratic but Andrew accepted this was the way things were going to be for a while. The literature on ADD makes clear that disrupted sleep patterns is one of the many complications – perhaps he had been lucky to have largely escaped this particular problem until now.

At last he was more open and willing to talk about his health. Our role was to keep him positive. We all hoped that things might improve once he was off the drugs for a longer period of time. While his illegal drug abuse was minimal or non existent as far as we knew, he was still putting a fair number of prescribed drugs into his system. It was difficult to know just how much these were helping him or if they were just compounding the problem. It was impossible to say and I suspect difficult for his doctor to gauge either.

At this time he found great solace in his other addiction - tobacco. He liked to roll his own and you knew how much they meant to him the way he pulled on his treasured product; the contortions on his face said it all – the psychiatrists can relate the need for nicotine to increased dopamine effectiveness in the brain – but as far as we were concerned it made him more relaxed; to us that was what mattered. Of course, smoking tobacco causes harm but it seemed the lesser evil. He drank quite a lot but probably no more than many of his age and was curtailed from regular excess by his lack of finances. Anyhow it seemed to do him good; after a few drinks he was always in good form.

Other ADD related symptoms started to appear or increase in intensity. He started to develop an infrequent, but noticeable, tremor in his arm or hand when pouring a drink or doing something similar. Poor motor co-ordination was another warning sign and reminded us of the stammer he had as a child. At that time he attended speech therapy and eventually the stammering largely disappeared, whether through intervention or not it was difficult to say. But it was also prone to return when he was under stress. The stammering was more noticeable now. At times you couldn't make out what he was saying.

He became accident prone. In the space of three weeks he had been in the same accident and emergency department of our local hospital three times. He had fallen over and broken a hand while lifting weights (another addiction but one that normally doesn't do any harm); he had fallen off a motor bike while being driven as a pillion passenger around some wasteland. Needless to say he didn't have any leathers on him and ended up covered with extensive scrapes and cuts – it was his luck to fall on the one small piece of tarmac in the area. On the third occasion he had driven into a low hanging branch on a country lane while out cycling on his bicycle in the dark and had broken his nose.

Around the same time his driving became very erratic - we agreed that he would not drive the car for the foreseeable future. The risk was just too great. We were just going to have to be patient and hope that he would come through this phase. I can remember reading that a common feature of ADD is that 'the individual engages in high risk activities with little thought of consequence or personal risk'. Andrew was proving to be almost archetypical in his presentation. It was also all too clear that an earlier hope that the effects of the ADD would be less apparent in adulthood was forlorn. Was it a case of simply replacing one worry with another?

He was attending follow-up consultations with his psychiatrist and she was trying to persuade him to attend counselling sessions. She was young and willing to confront issues head on. I had met her when accompanying Andrew to A&E following one of his accidents. I suggested that Andrew should be admitted as an in – patient for a period of time to get him through the current crisis. Regrettably, this was not possible – he did not meet the criteria for 'sectioning' as he was not thought to be a risk to others and crucially would not give his consent. Our inability to do something was debilitating.

Nonetheless, there were good days mixed in with the bad and as long as you accepted the limitations he was becoming easier to live with in the home. Certainly, with careful handling confrontations could be reduced to a minimum. We all hoped that the current crisis was a blip. We were worried about his health but at least we, and him, did not have the black cloud hanging over us that had been there for the previous years. We could try to be optimistic.

I think by now we realised that he was always going to need looked after to at least some extent. When planning holidays we knew that we either took Andrew with us or would not leave him for too long on his own. He was fine on his own for short spells. We could only hope that in due course he would get involved in a relationship with the type of girl who could meet his needs. A return to employment and the right partner could work wonders. Perhaps, it is wishful thinking hoping that at some stage the worry could be shared by someone else.

Epilogue

You can walk into most good bookshops and find a book on ADD, or ADHD to give it its more common name. Some of the biggest sellers even have a complete section devoted to the condition. Most of the titles seem to be written by experts in the field – doctors, psychologists, teachers or the like. There is the odd one written by a parent who is now active in this or that charity related to the condition. I often have a quick flick through this section when I visit a good bookstore. It's hard not to smile as the pages are turned. Chapters on the identification of ADHD or its biological origins abound, as do tips for coping with the condition in the home or in the classroom; all good common sense. But I've yet to find something that focuses on the long term wreckage that must be all too common. Maybe that type of book doesn't make commercial sense or perhaps it's a condition that requires blind optimism. Readers, invariably parents, no doubt, seeking a book on this topic don't want to leave the shop in despair. The books, in general, are beacons of hope.

Yet, for so many and for so often there seems little hope. The almost daily battles in the home, the searching the streets, the trashed car – perhaps because some shady drug dealer was owed money, the phone being cut off when we were on holiday because a gambling hotline using premium numbers was in use throughout the night, the drug addiction, the inevitable sliding into trouble with the police are all part of the same picture of despair. Events all too common for so many parents in general, and parents of ADHD children in particular.

ADHD leaves no member of an affected family unscathed.

Only one member may have the condition but the others also pay the price. Sarah's long battle with depression may not be due to Andrew's ADHD; she had previous episodes before he was born but there is little doubt that it played its part. She has been left fragile and can succumb without warning to the most unpredictable trigger. Chaos can emerge out of calmness like the flick of a switch.

In recent months, Sarah has found it difficult to go out to social events. Hearing about other 'wonderful' children delivered with a typical lack of sensitivity by life-shielded mothers took its toll. She simply stopped going out. It's too early to say if she will ever return to what once passed as normal.

Men tend to cope better; we can distance ourselves from the emotional baggage. Some author's suggest that we can compartmentalise our feelings and only address inner turmoil at the times when we have the mental resources to cope. It's difficult to say how I have been affected. Perhaps I'm better equipped for any further traumas life can throw my direction. But it probably has done some damage. Recurring bouts of gastritis, duodenitis, and oesophagitis are stress related or so I was told, and they have peaked over the last year. Medication for this includes proton pump inhibitors that slow the outpouring of acid from the stomach wall. At times of deepest pain I could almost feel the acid being secreted as my stomach churned. Stomach churning moments don't need to be imagined; they are all too real and all too often.

Perhaps it was the months of waiting for the police car to arrive at the door or the summons to be delivered that caused the most stress. The sound of every car slowing down as it passed our house had its cumulative effect; experiences beyond the wildest imagination of most parents.

For some, difficult times lead to an embracing of religion.

How could it not have the opposite effect? Where was the omnipotent and benevolent God that we hear and read so much about? There is not much benevolence in being born with the genes that lead to ADHD. There is not much to write home about being a parent of a child so disabled. If it is part of some master plan it is a plan beyond comprehension. No, Dawkins and company are right. We are at the mercy of natural selection and our genes. It is pot luck. Good parenting is important but so much depends on the meiotic dice.

Mental health services have long been under-resourced. Chronic psychiatric conditions such as ADHD are even further down the queue. Memories of our visits to the GP 10-12 years ago and our engagement with the clinical psychologist around the same time are still difficult to reconcile. Neither of them had mentioned the condition at that time. They probably weren't aware of it. Things may be better now but I suspect not that much better. More knowledge may be there but progress is still slow due to limited resources. There is probably still more trial and error with psychiatry and its allies than with other medical specialities. Can psychiatrists necessarily achieve a lot more than a pharmacist with good counselling skills? Fixing the mal-aligned brain is a bit more complex than removing a gall bladder.

Schools are still the place where the condition impacts most apart from in the home. Many schools have valiant staff members who try to identify and support the children with this unforgiving condition. Often they are unsupported and under-resourced. Others simply write these pupils off as being 'bad boys' or blame the parenting. ADHD is not a fashionable cause, there are not too many street or school collections raising money to find a cause or cure.

Perhaps it is the many misconceptions about the condition

that does the damage. Rarely a week goes by without some feature writer in the press referring to ADD as the medicalision of poor behaviour, often attributed to weak and inconsistent parenting. It is probable that some GP's are all too willing to attach the label of ADD to some children when it is not really justified, particularly if under pressure from the parents to give a medical justification to poor behaviour, or a child out of control, or even to support an application for Disability Living Allowance. This may mean that in Britain it is a condition that is possibly over-diagnosed and it is this that creates the bad press. However, over-diagnosis, if it exists, does not mean that the condition is not real; those who claim this are ignorant in the true sense of the word and clearly unaware of the scientific research that has already taken place.

Perhaps this is what instils the sense of isolation for many of those affected by the condition and their carers. It is bad enough having the condition without half the population not believing that it exists. Many mothers gain support through contacts made on support websites. For many this support can be a lifeline; I know that for Sarah it has on occasions been what has kept her going.

The judicial process itself can add to the strain. While having AHDH is not a fast track to a criminal lifestyle it dramatically increases the chances of some contact with the law enforcement agencies. An impulsive or addictive personality invites trouble. In Andrew's case, the two year period from crime to sentence allowed an opportunity to reflect and try to achieve some stability. The long wait was a sentence in itself for all concerned. The knowledge that a high proportion of people in penal institutions are suffering from some form of mental illness doesn't make you feel any better either – would it not be as cost effective, and ethically more desirable, to channel more resources into better mental health care for those with conditions that may be helped? Does society in general really want to know or care?

The tension now is much reduced and there are genuinely good times but there is still darkness. The underlying condition is still there; impulsiveness is still there but now less likely to cause sparks in the home. It manifests itself in impulsive buying – buying that new bike that may only get used for a few weeks, or that new shirt, or his tenth pair of expensive denims, or those concert tickets even though getting there is not practical. We always know if Andrew was the last person to use the microwave; the door will have been opened, the food removed and eaten, before the timer had run down. Organisation skills are still dire but we are now more able to support him as he is more willing to be supported. We all accept that we must write his lists and send him his reminders, check his bank account and check that the bills are paid. Empathy is still a foreign land and one that is unlikely to ever be on his list of tourist destinations. Perhaps we have changed as well. Our expectations are more realistic and we accept that things are different; that things are not always done as we would like them to be. Is this because we have become more accepting or is it that we simply have been ground down?

It is hard not to be affected by self–doubt at times. Did we do all that we could? Was the balance between holding the line and backing off as good as it could have been? Were we too accepting of the damage done to others in our desire to do all we could for Andrew? Would he have fared better if we had forced him to live independently in recent years? Our world contains many 'What ifs?' Not knowing the answers can add to the strain. What would other parents have done in the same position? No one can really understand unless they have walked the same path.

At 25 where is Andrew now - disabled in the wider sense of the word? We are long past the stage of trying to analyse the respective roles of genetics and poor choices in the condition. Is there a difference or are the two not really different sides of the same coin. It is OK for the righteous to talk about free will but for many the will is not as 'free' as it is for others and is skewed by the unfortunate out-workings of the genetic lottery.

Moralisers tend not to have visited the depths of despair.

But he is trying to move ahead. He may be out of work but he has enrolled on a HND course in Construction at the local college. He understands the importance of increasing his chances of getting work when the upturn eventually comes; particularly if there is no work around at present. And a student loan will help pay the bills. The 9 to 5 routine will also give him focus and a greater sense of purpose.

His relationships with his sisters are at an all time high. He discusses his condition with Suzanne and they talk about the trivial things that brothers and sisters the world over do. There is an obvious warmth between them; a warmth that wasn't always evident in the darkest days. He is very close to Rebecca. Not surprising when they both live in the same house and are far enough apart in age to avoid the sibling rivalries that often exist. He is almost a surrogate father figure to her, protecting and caring. Yet, in terms of maturity there is probably not that much difference between them.

The worst may or may not be over; it is difficult to predict where we will be even a few weeks further down the line, let alone have a longer term view There will still be difficult challenges ahead, for him and for us. But now we have understanding where once there was only despair.

20 July 2009

Postscript

Six days after completing this account of Andrew's battle against ADD, and its myriad of complications, he was dead. He choked in his sleep and the autopsy confirmed that there were small amounts of alcohol, prescription and recreational drugs in his system. Not enough of anything to kill him on its own, or even in combination, but enough to depress his coughing reflex at a critical time. Yet again, he had run out of luck – if he hadn't taken the sleeping pill or had gone to sleep on his side instead of his back?

Attention Deficit Disorder may not have been written on his death certificate but it might as well have been. Would he have been depressed or drug dependent if he had not had the condition? Would he have been so reckless in mixing what he had taken?

Living with Andrew was a rollercoaster ride and often difficult - we all fought his battles with him. If only there had been early diagnosis and intervention, how different it all could have been; living with this knowledge is now one of **our** battles.

I am completing the writing of this section on my birthday. There is no card from Andrew – not that there are any cards as such – the phrase 'Happy Birthday' is all too incongruous. Yet it is a poignant time. Andrew's card from last year is still in the bottom drawer of my bedside cabinet. For the past few years, I have kept his most recent card in the same drawer until the next one arrived, aware, perhaps subconsciously, that each one could be the last. Perhaps, the transient nature of his life had become all too predictable.

However, nothing has prepared us for the pain of his loss.

"first day of new school yday ……. Mum says u wudav been proud but I reckon ud just av been like "aw well wait til u hear bout my day"

Miss u Andi!! Love Becca xxxxxxxxxxxxxxxxxxxxxxxxxxxx xxxxxxxxxxxxxxxxxxxxxxxxxxxxxxxxxxxxxxxxxxxxxxxxxx xxxxxxxxxxxxxxxxxxxxxxxxxxxxxxxxxxx